HELLO, CUPCAKE!
WHAT'S NEW?

HELLO, CUPCAKE!

WHAT'S NEW?

Karen Tack and Alan Richardson

HOUGHTON MIFFLIN HARCOURT
Boston New York 2011

To my mom and dad, who believe that
every meal should end with dessert—even breakfast.
—K.T.

In memory of my mom, who never cooked
a meal she didn't like—and she was right.
—A.R.

Library of Congress Cataloging-in-Publication Data
Tack, Karen.
Hello, cupcake! what's new? / Karen Tack and Alan Richardson
  p. cm.
  "Selections previously published in a different form as What's New, Cupcake? copyright © 2010 by Karen Tack and Alan Richardson and Hello, Cupcake! copyright © 2008 by Karen Tack and Alan Richardson"—Prelim.
  ISBN 978-0-547-57955-9
  1. Cupcakes. 2. Cake decorating.
  3. Cookbooks. I. Richardson, Alan, date.
II. Richardson, Alan, date. Hello, cupcake!
III. Richardson, Alan, date. What's new, cupcake?
IV. Title.
TX771.T32 2011
641.8'653—dc22
2010036729

Acknowledgments

So many people helped make *Hello, Cupcake!* a success, and so many more helped us to create *What's New, Cupcake?* We are lucky to have families that are both patient and talented. The Tack family has lived with cupcakes and candy up to their eyeballs for countless months. Chris Tack supports us, cheers us on, and advises us on every project, every step of the way. Erik and Liam Tack mostly assist by ignoring our insanity but also chime in with the necessary "Awesome!" when we get it right. We rely on Larry Frascella as our trusted in-house barometer, always letting us know when our cupcakes are too weird or when our words don't make sense. Thanks to all of you for everything—we love you.

Our support team at our publishing house has been amazing. We have an insightful editor, Rux Martin, who keeps us on our toes at all times. We are also grateful to Rux and her partner, Barry Estabrook, for letting Elvis and Presley, their dachshunds, pose for our cupcakes. We are grateful to Colby Lawrence for her efforts in making this new edition possible. Our art director, Michaela Sullivan, always makes our work look gorgeous, and this new edition is no exception. Thanks also to Anne Chalmers, Eugenie Delaney, and Rebecca Springer for their tremendous work on our books. Our amazing marketing and publicity team, Lori Glazer, Katrina Kruse, and Megan Wilson, has brought us to heights we never expected. Steve Quinn, Casey Whalen, Ron Hussey, Jacinta Monniere, Valerie Cimino, Susan Dickinson, Gail Cohen, and so many others, we couldn't do it without you.

A special thanks to friends Richard and Sherry Zucker for coming along on our cupcake ride and for the incisive ideas offered to us throughout the making and marketing of both books. Many thanks to our friend Deb Donahue for rescuing us with props whenever we started to run low.

We don't know if Martha Kaplan is the wisest agent on earth or the most diligent nanny, but either way she seems to always be watching out for us. We can't thank you enough, Martha.

We have had terrific support from so many surprising sources. Kathie Lee Gifford and Hoda Kotb at *Today* have been on the cupcake train from the beginning. Producer Brian Balthazar was an early believer and did so much to help us. Paula Deen and Brandon Branch have been amazingly generous with their support. Sandy Ploy, Rachel Bussel, and Nichelle Stephens blog their joy in cupcaking every day, and we are grateful they have taken us along for the ride. To Dorie Greenspan, Carol Prager, Maria McBride, Doug Turshen, Mark Bittman, Susan Westmoreland, Linda Fears, Karmen Lizzul, Jane Chestnut, Jackie Plant, Sally Lee, Babs Chernetz, Beth Lipton, Karen Cicero, Marisol Vera, Catherine Cassidy, Ardith Cope, Barbara Schuetz, Sarah Thompson, Stephanie Saible, Chris Koury, Karen Tanaka, and so many more friends in our publishing family, thank you for your support and for making sure our cupcakes never lost their creative edge. We appreciate everything you've done.

And to all the wonderful readers, eaters, and new friends who have welcomed our cupcakes into their homes, hearts, and yes, stomachs, all we can say is thank you. Every time we hear your cupcake stories, it gives us a thrill. So cheers to you all, and keep on cupcaking.

CONTENTS

Introduction 1

Cupcaking Materials,
Tools, and Techniques 5

April Fool's Play 22

Happy Birthday, Cupcake! 52

I Thought You Ordered
Chocolate Moose 84

Let's Party, Cupcake! 116

The House That Boo Built 152

Hooray for Holly Days 186

Cupcakes, Frostings, and Cookies 218

Sources 226

Cupcake Index 228

Introduction

With just a handful of candies, a can of frosting, a ziplock bag, and some cupcake batter, you are on your way to putting tasty tuxedos on a parade of marching penguins, planting a garden of spring vegetables so sweet even the kids will eat them, or turning your next pool party into a shark attack. When the mailman tires of your snarling dog, meet him at the end of the drive with a terrier cupcake before he goes postal. If your son brings home a D in biology, send him to school with a platter of insect cupcakes to show he's ready to get down to business. Want to see the inside of your new neighbor's house? Send her a bouquet of sunflower cupcakes to break the ice.

Make our cupcakes for a holiday or a special event, and they'll provide the entertainment. Play an April Fool's trick on the family with a cupcake dinner of spaghetti and meatballs. At the neighborhood Halloween party, hand out alien cupcakes oozing with neon frosting and sitting in their own spaceships. When you want a little more sophistication, our patterned cupcakes are refined enough to serve with champagne.

All this is easy: honest. Forget the complicated pastry techniques and expensive decorating supplies. You can find almost everything for these projects at your local grocery store, drugstore, or even a gas-station convenience store (which often has some of the most extensive selections of candies). M&Ms work equally well as noses, eyes, or ears. A circus peanut candy transforms into a horse's head or a koi goldfish. For finishing your designs, a ziplock bag makes a great disposable piping bag.

You don't need any baking skills to make these projects either. We've given you lots of EZ Cupcakes, including beautiful mums for Mother's Day and pies for a bake sale that will make you look like the most talented pastry chef around. We show you how to doctor store-bought cake mixes with flavors like chocolate-mint and orange-spice. No one will suspect you didn't make these cupcakes from scratch, and they have a uniformly firm surface that won't pull apart when you frost them. And as for the frosting, we have yet to find a homemade version that has the versatility of canned. Store-bought frostings take well to tinting, making it simple to create vibrant colors, and are perfect for microwaving, melting into a consistently smooth texture for dipping. For a silky smooth finish with a personal touch, we have also included our patented "almost-homemade" buttercream frosting in eight flavors, from espresso to raspberry.

So what's new, Cupcake? Turn a page, pick a project, grab a bag or two of candy, and get ready to put your smile into overdrive. It's time to get this party started.

So many ways to decorate . . .

With so many ways to use candy to decorate a cupcake, there's never a reason to be without an ingredient. Need a leaf? Try green Swedish Fish, spearmint leaves, or a candy fruit slice. Haven't got a stem? You can make almost anything from taffy. Check the pantry and fire up your imagination.

Try a candy swap

Flower Power (page 65)

Anatomy of an CUPCAKE

A few ingredients
+ simple techniques
= cupcakes anyone can make.

(You'll find EZ Cupcakes in every chapter.)

Cupcaking Materials, Tools, and Techniques

Koi Pond (page 99)

Bake-Sale Pies (page 42)

Ants on a Picnic (page 102)

Designer Candies

Small, colorful candies are perfect for creating a border, outlining a shape, or making a whimsical design.

Alternate colors to create a border.

Arrange in abstract patterns.

Create whimsical mosaics.

Mimic animals and objects.

Roller Candies

Taffy, chews, and sugared jellies are soft enough to be combined, shaped, rolled, and cut, giving them limitless design possibilities.

• Place taffy in the microwave for no more than 3 seconds to soften.

• Combine and roll out taffy to make thin sheets of colorful candy.

• Roll out jellies in sugar, using more sugar on top as needed to prevent sticking.

• Combine spice drops or jellies to make larger shapes.

• Cut with scissors, pinking shears, cookie cutters, or a paring knife.

Flex Candies

Flexible candies can be twisted, bent, or cut to make fanciful designs.

Tie knots, bend, and shape.

Cut fruit rolls to create flat shapes with color.

Snip or cut marshmallows, gum, and Circus Peanuts.

Essential Tools for Cupcaking

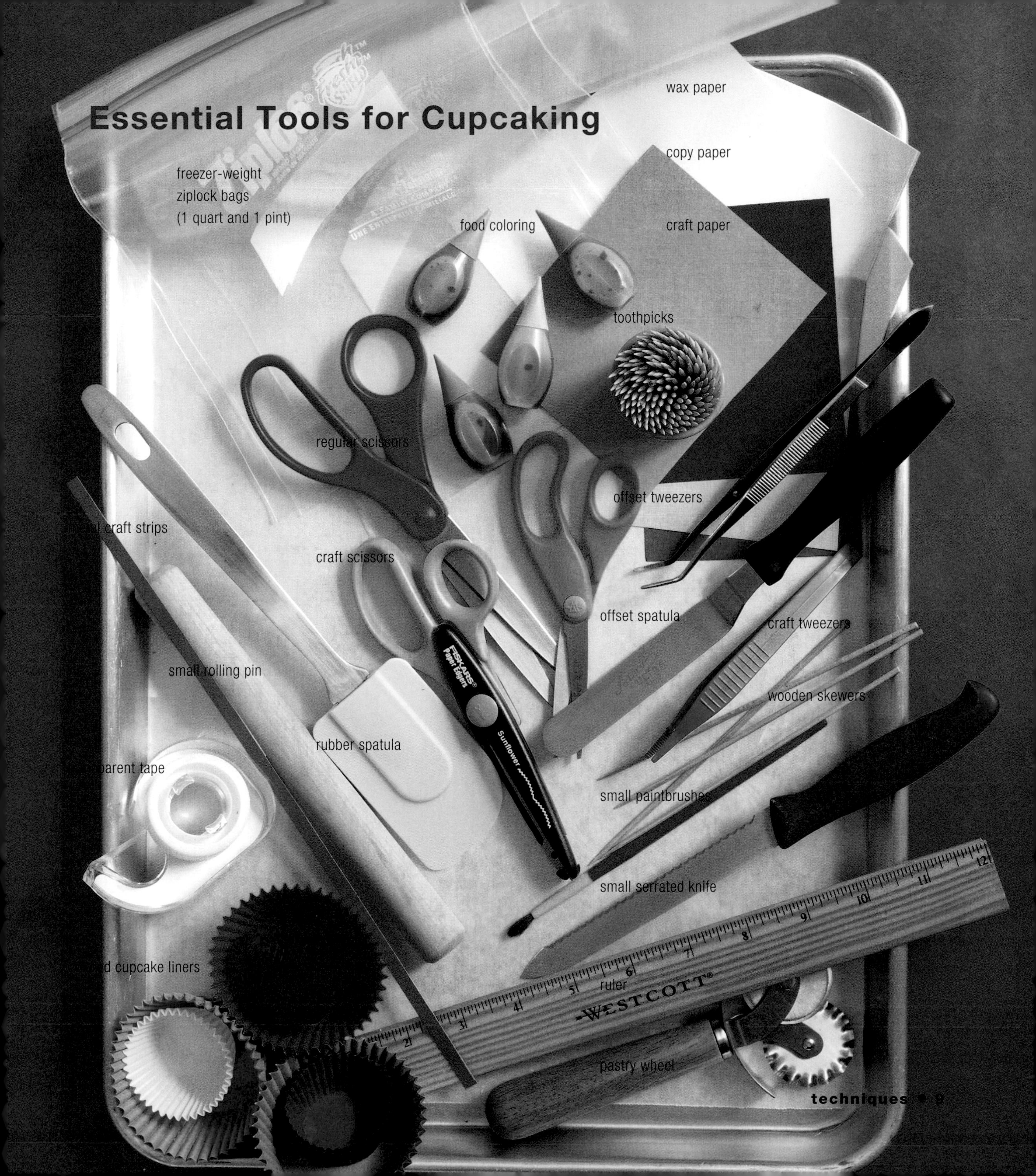

freezer-weight
ziplock bags
(1 quart and 1 pint)

food coloring

wax paper

copy paper

craft paper

toothpicks

regular scissors

offset tweezers

craft scissors

offset spatula

metal craft strips

craft tweezers

small rolling pin

wooden skewers

rubber spatula

FISKARS
Paper Edgers

Sunflower

transparent tape

small paintbrushes

small serrated knife

foil cupcake liners

ruler

pastry wheel

WESTCOTT

Filling Cupcake Liners

To avoid dribbling batter and to make it easy to get the same amount in every paper liner, use a freezer-weight ziplock bag.

• Use two 1-quart freezer-weight ziplock bags to hold 1 standard recipe mix.

• Place ziplock bags in separate plastic containers large enough to support them and fold the edges back over the containers.

• Divide the batter evenly between the bags, press out the excess air, and seal.

• Grasp the bag below the zipper, push the batter down to one corner, and snip $1/2$ inch from the corner.

• Put the cut opening in the center of a liner, squeeze gently, fill two-thirds full, stop squeezing, lift, and repeat with the remaining liners.

• Use a rubber spatula to squeegee the last of the batter down to the corner for piping.

Frosting Cupcakes

For a smooth experience, keep the frosting at room temperature and stir before using. And remember, less is never more.

Start by mounding a large dollop in the center and push to the edges.

Push the frosting in one direction while turning the cupcake in the opposite direction.

Swipe the top to remove any excess frosting and smooth the top.

For a peak, use the tip of an offset spatula to swirl and lift the frosting.

Filling a Ziplock Bag

Be sure to use freezer-weight bags because they can take the pressure when you squeeze.

• Invert the bag over your open hand and press to make a cup inside your fingers.

• Fill the cup inside your fingers with frosting and then lift the edges of the bag up and around the frosting.

• Press out the excess air and seal the bag.

• Use scissors to snip a corner according to the recipe.

Piping Frosting

THE SQUEEZE-RELEASE-PULL TECHNIQUE FOR GRASS, FUR, PETALS, AND TEETH

Touch the tip of the bag to the surface, squeeze, and anchor the frosting. Release the pressure before lifting. Pull away to make a peak.

THE ANCHOR-FLY-ANCHOR TECHNIQUE FOR "FLYING" STRAIGHT LINES

Touch the tip of the bag to the surface, squeeze, and anchor the frosting. Pull up and away while continuing to squeeze, creating a "flying" straight line. Let the line drop into place, stop squeezing, and anchor it at the end.

 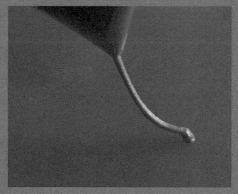 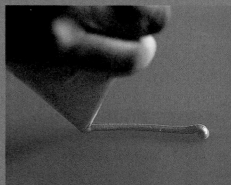

THE SQUEEZE-DRAG TECHNIQUE FOR BEADING

Touch the tip of the bag to the surface, squeeze a dot, and drag it. Lift the tip and return directly next to the first dot. Squeeze another dot and drag it, repeating in a straight line to make beading.

Building Cupcake Shapes

Snacks and candies hidden under the frosting of our cupcakes give them unexpected shapes.

Use a marshmallow, doughnut hole, and cupcake for a duck.

Frost the cupcake and press the shapes into the frosting.

Fill in the gaps at the edges and place in the freezer to chill.

Coating Cupcakes

After chilling, cupcakes can be finished any way you choose.

Cover with frosting for a textured look.

Coat in coconut for a fuzzy look.

Dip in melted frosting for a shiny look.

Dipping Cupcakes

Dipping cupcakes in melted canned frosting is one of those techniques that look amazingly sophisticated but are really easy to do. Canned frostings hold up well to heat and firm up nicely into a smooth sheen when they cool. Avoid the low-sugar or whipped varieties, as they tend to fall apart when heated.

Microwave the frosting according to the recipe. The best test for texture is to dip a spoon into the frosting and let it run back into the cup. It should have the texture of lightly whipped cream.

Chill the cupcake assemblies first to keep them from separating in the warm frosting. Hold a chilled cupcake by its paper bottom and dip the top into the melted frosting as directed in the recipe.

Use a spoon to ladle additional frosting over hard-to-reach areas. Lift the cupcake and allow the excess frosting to drip off before inverting and placing it aside to set.

Tinting Sugars, Nonpareils, Sprinkles, and Coconut

• Place the sugar, nonpareils, sprinkles, coconut, or other material in a ziplock bag.

• Add a few drops of food coloring to the bag. You can create new colors by mixing basic colors, like yellow and red to make orange.

• Seal the bag and shake until the sugar or other ingredient is evenly tinted.

Spread the tinted ingredient on wax paper to dry.

Store dried tinted sugar or other items in a sealed container until ready to use.

Edging and Coating Cupcakes

TO EDGE
A CUPCAKE

Place the coating material in a shallow bowl large enough to accommodate the cupcake. Hold the bowl at an angle and gently roll the edge in the coating material.

TO COAT
A CUPCAKE

Lightly press the frosting into the coating material to coat and shape the entire surface.

Drawing with Chocolate

Candy melting wafers melt and harden just like chocolate and are easier to handle. They come in a variety of colors and make custom shapes and designs a cinch.

• Place the chocolate melting wafers in a ziplock bag; do not seal. Microwave for 10 seconds, check to be sure the bag is not too hot to handle, massage the bag to smooth the chocolate, and microwave for another 10 seconds, massaging to remove all lumps. Repeat as necessary.

• Press out the excess air, seal the bag, and push the melted candy down to one corner.

• Snip off a small corner of the ziplock bag as directed in the recipe.

• Place wax paper over the template, pipe the outline of the template, and then fill in the center of the shape.

• Tap the work surface gently to settle and smooth the chocolate drawing.

Add decorations such as nonpareils before the chocolate hardens.

Use a back-and-forth motion to create zigzag patterns for pine needles.

Supports for Candies and Cookies

Sandwich a pretzel between vanilla wafers using melted white chocolate for the glue.

Glue pretzels to the back of a cookie using melted chocolate.

Push pretzels directly into soft candies like spice drops and soft taffy.

Glue pretzels together using melted white chocolate to make a split-rail fence.

Press pretzels into cookie dough before baking, and bake in place.

Cupcaking with Custom Cookie Shapes

• Start with store-bought sugar cookie or chocolate cookie dough from the refrigerator case. (See Quick Sugar Cookie recipes, page 225.)

• Incorporate flour (for sugar cookies) or unsweetened cocoa powder (for chocolate cookies) and roll out on wax paper.

• Cut out the cookies, transfer to a cookie sheet, and bake according to the package directions.

To make simple shapes, or if you need only a few cookies, use a small knife to follow the template and cut out the cookies.

For more intricate shapes, or when you need a lot of cookies, bend 1/2-inch metal strips (available at craft stores) into shapes to match the templates and tape the ends to create custom cookie cutters.

Lids, straws, and other common kitchen items can also be useful for cutting cookies.

Cupcaking with Melted Hard Candy

- Place the candies in a freezer-weight ziplock bag.

- Use the back of a pan, a rolling pin, or a hammer to break the candy into small, but not powder-fine, pieces.

- Place the crushed candy in an even layer on a foil-lined cookie sheet and bake in a 350°F oven until just melted and smooth, 3 to 4 minutes.

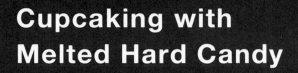

- While the candy is still soft, press oiled metal cutters into it, leave them in place, and allow to cool completely.

- Gently break the shapes from the cooled candy sheet.

You can also fill prebaked cookie shapes with crushed candy and bake for a few minutes more to melt the candy.

April Fool's Play

French fries from pound cake, a banana with crunch, foot-longs with spice drops and taffy for lunch. Lo mein with fruit chews may sound gourmet, but think twice before eating—it's April Fool's Day. These cupcakes are the perfect foil for birthdays, holidays, sleepovers, or any time you need a laugh.

Side of Fries   24

Bagels and Lox   26

Hold the Anchovies   28

Faux Foot-Long   31

All Cracked Up   35

Corn on the Cob   38

Spaghetti and Meatballs   40

Bake-Sale Pies   42

Chinese Takeout   44

Banana Split   49

vanilla frosting

pound cake

red food coloring

SIDE OF FRIES

ez
CUPCAKE

Want fries with that? Our clever crinkle-cuts are made from pound cake lightly toasted to look as though they're right out of the fryer. If you prefer straight-cut fries, just slice them into long, thin strips and toast them up. Squirt on the frosting ketchup, and these fries are ready for the drive-up window.

> 4 **mini vanilla cupcakes baked in white paper liners**
> 10 **vanilla cupcakes baked in white paper liners**
>
> 1 **frozen pound cake (10.75 ounces; Sara Lee), thawed**
> 1 **can (16 ounces) vanilla frosting**
> **Red food coloring (use paste coloring for a darker red; Wilton)**
> **Plastic squeeze bottle (optional)**
> **Extra red frosting for ketchup bottle (optional)**

1. Trim the ends of the pound cake. Cut the pound cake into ½-inch-thick slices. Using a crinkle vegetable cutter (see Sources), cut the pound cake crosswise into ½-inch-wide strips. Transfer the strips to two cookie sheets and spread in a single layer.

2. Preheat the broiler to high. Toast the pound cake strips under the broiler until golden, 20 to 30 seconds. Turn the pieces and continue toasting until all sides are golden. Repeat with the other cookie sheet. Transfer to a wire rack to cool.

3. Tint ¼ cup of the vanilla frosting bright red with the red food coloring. For the ketchup, spread the red frosting on top of the mini cupcakes and smooth. Spread the tops of the standard cupcakes with the

remaining vanilla frosting to cover. Arrange the cooled fries on top of the vanilla-frosted standard cupcakes, 4 to 6 fries per cupcake. Arrange the cupcakes in a cardboard container or on a platter with the red-frosted mini cupcakes. Serve with more red frosting in a squeeze bottle, if desired.

BAGELS AND LOX

Where's the Sunday paper? This bagel is a mini doughnut with a schmear of vanilla frosting. Add a slice of orange fruit-chew lox, sprinkle with scallions of green licorice, and serve with a wedge of candy lemon on the side.

24 **vanilla cupcakes baked in pale yellow paper liners (see Sources)**

24 **plain mini doughnuts**

 2 **tablespoons light corn syrup**

 1 **tablespoon poppy seeds**

24 **orange fruit chews (Starburst)**

 1 **can (16 ounces) vanilla frosting**

Yellow food coloring

 4 **strands green licorice twists (Twizzlers Rainbow Twists), thinly sliced diagonally**

24 **mini candy lemon slices**

1. Cut the doughnuts in half horizontally to make the bagels. Heat the corn syrup in a small bowl in the microwave until bubbly, 5 to 10 seconds. Brush the top of the doughnuts with the corn syrup. Sprinkle lightly with the poppy seeds and set aside.

2. Soften several orange fruit chews at a time in the microwave for 2 to 3 seconds. Roll out each fruit chew on a sheet of wax paper to a $2^1/_2$-by-$1^1/_4$-inch rectangle. Score the top lengthwise with a knife.

3. Spread a thin layer of the vanilla frosting on the cut side of the bottom half of each doughnut. Arrange 1 fruit chew, folded slightly to look like lox, on top.

4. Tint the remaining vanilla frosting yellow with the food coloring and spread on top of the cupcakes. Place the bottom half of 1 doughnut on each cupcake. Scatter a few licorice slices over the doughnut and place 1 doughnut half with poppy seeds on top. Serve with a candy lemon slice on the side.

HOLD THE ANCHOVIES

One large pizza to go. Pile on the pepperoni (fruit leather), bring on the sausage (chocolate cookies), don't forget the sauce (red frosting)—and make it with extra cheese (grated white chocolate). And be sure to brown that crust with cocoa powder.

19 **vanilla cupcakes baked in white paper liners**

8 **ounces white chocolate chips**

1 **can (16 ounces) plus 1/2 cup vanilla frosting**

1 **teaspoon unsweetened cocoa powder**

Yellow and red food coloring (use paste color for a darker red; Wilton)

2 **rolls strawberry fruit leather (Fruit by the Foot)**

10 **thin chocolate cookies (Famous Chocolate Wafers)**

1/3 **cup chocolate-covered raisins (Raisinets)**

1 **package (0.9 ounce) small round chocolate cookies (Gripz)**

1 **medium pizza box (optional)**

1. Melt the white chocolate chips in a microwavable bowl in the microwave for about 1 minute, stopping to stir frequently, until smooth. Spoon the melted chocolate into a small plastic or foil container (about 2 by 4 inches and 2 inches deep). Smooth the top and refrigerate until set, about 20 minutes. When set, remove from the container and let stand at room temperature.

2. Tint 1 1/4 cups of the vanilla frosting light brown with 1/2 teaspoon of the cocoa powder and a few drops of yellow food coloring. Spoon the frosting into a zip-lock bag, press out the excess air, and seal. Tint the remaining 3/4 cup frosting red with the food coloring. Place the red frosting in a microwavable bowl; cover with plastic wrap.

3. For the pepperoni, cut the fruit leather into as many 1-inch circles as possible using the back of a pastry tip, a small cookie cutter, or scissors. For the cheese, place a box grater on top of a sheet of wax paper and grate about half of the block of white chocolate on the largest openings.

4. Arrange the cupcakes on a serving platter or in a pizza box (we ask our local pizza parlor for a pizza box; we get it for free). Place 1 cupcake in the center. Surround the cupcake with 6 more cupcakes and surround those with the 12 remaining cupcakes to make a pizza-size circle. Press the cupcakes as close together as possible.

5. Using a serrated knife, cut 6 of the chocolate wafer cookies in half. Using scissors, snip a small corner from the bag with the light brown frosting. Pipe a small amount of frosting on each corner of the cookie semicircle and use frosting to adhere the cookie, rounded side out, between 2 cupcakes on the outer edge. Repeat to fill in all the gaps, making a continuous outer edge. Cut the remaining 4 wafer cookies into pieces that will cover any of the remaining openings in the center of the cupcake assembly to make a solid surface. Attach the cookie pieces with a small amount of frosting.

6. Snip a larger ($\frac{1}{2}$-inch) corner from the bag with the light brown frosting. For the crust, pipe a steady line of frosting along the outer edge. Use a small spatula to blend the inside edge of the frosting crust onto the cupcakes.

7. Microwave the red frosting to soften slightly, 3 to 5 seconds. For the sauce, spoon the red frosting in the center of the cupcake circle and spread to the edge of the crust circle, creating a few swirls for texture.

8. Sprinkle the top of the red frosting with the grated white chocolate. Arrange the fruit leather pepperoni all over. For the sausage, add the chocolate-covered raisins and the small chocolate cookies in small clusters. Grate more white chocolate, if desired. Place the remaining $\frac{1}{2}$ teaspoon cocoa powder in a fine sieve and lightly dust a few areas on the crust for that pizza-oven color.

Makes 1 foot-long hero,
4 cupcakes

FAUX FOOT-LONG

Twelve inches of deli-fresh ham, cheese, lettuce, tomato, onion, and pickles layered on a seeded hero says April Fool's as only candy can. Our meat and cheese are made from fruit chews, the onions are cut from spice drops, the tomato is a fruit slice, and the lettuce leaves are cereal flakes tossed in green frosting. The hero itself? Cake doughnut sticks with sesame seeds.

4 vanilla cupcakes baked in white paper liners

1 cup corn or rice cereal flakes

1 cup canned vanilla frosting

Green food coloring

8 yellow fruit chews (Laffy Taffy, Starburst, Tootsie Fruit Rolls)

12 pink fruit chews (Laffy Taffy, Starburst, Jolly Rancher)

2 red candy fruit slices

2 tablespoons granulated sugar

6 white spice drops

2 plain cake doughnut sticks (6–8 inches long; Dunkin' Donuts)

1 teaspoon light corn syrup

2 teaspoons sesame seeds

3 green gumdrops (Dots)

Crispy apple chips (Seneca; optional)

1. Place the cereal in a medium bowl. Spoon 1 tablespoon vanilla frosting into a small ziplock bag, press out the excess air, and seal. Tint ¼ cup of the vanilla frosting green with the green food coloring. Heat the green frosting in a microwavable bowl in the microwave, stopping to stir frequently, until it has the texture of lightly whipped cream, about 15 seconds. Pour the frosting over the

cereal and toss well to coat. Spread the coated cereal on a cookie sheet in an even layer and refrigerate until set, about 15 minutes.

2. For the cheese, microwave the yellow fruit chews for 2 to 3 seconds to soften. Press 2 fruit chews together and roll out on a clean work surface into a rectangle about $\frac{1}{8}$ inch thick. Cut into a $1\frac{1}{2}$-by-2 inch rectangle. Continue with the remaining yellow fruit chews, rerolling scraps, to make a total of 6 rectangles. For the holes in the cheese, cut out small circles in the rectangles using an apple corer, a pastry tip, or a small round cookie cutter. For the ham, microwave the pink fruit chews for 2 to 3 seconds to soften. Press 2 fruit chews together and roll out on a clean work surface into a circle about $\frac{1}{8}$ inch thick. Cut each circle in half to make 12 semicircles.

3. For the tomatoes, cut each red fruit slice in half crosswise to make 2 thin slices. Sprinkle the work surface with some of the granulated sugar. For the onions, roll out the white spice drops $\frac{1}{8}$ inch thick, adding more sugar as necessary to prevent sticking. Cut out $\frac{1}{8}$-inch-wide onion rings using various sizes of small round cookie cutters, lids, pastry tips, or scissors, making as many rings as you can cut. For the hero-roll tops, cut $\frac{1}{2}$ inch from the bottom of the doughnut sticks; discard the bottom portion. Place the trimmed doughnut sticks, cut side down, on the work surface and cut each crosswise into two $2\frac{1}{2}$- to 3-inch pieces. Remove $\frac{1}{4}$ inch from the rounded ends of 2 of the pieces. Brush the tops with the corn syrup and sprinkle with the sesame seeds. For the pickle slices, flatten the green gumdrops with a rolling pin into rounds. Trim the edges with a small scalloped cookie cutter or decorative scissors. For the pickle seeds, snip a very small corner from the bag with the vanilla frosting and pipe small white dots in the center of each pickle slice.

4. Spread the tops of the cupcakes with the remaining vanilla frosting. Arrange the green cereal along the outer edge of the cupcakes as the lettuce. Add a red fruit slice as the tomato and a few onion rings made of spice drops to each cupcake. Add a few slices of cheese. Gather the straight sides of the pink fruit chews to create wavy ham slices and place on top of the cheese slices. Arrange the cupcakes in a row on a serving platter. Top with the doughnut sticks, untrimmed rounded pieces at the ends, to make the bread. Serve with the pickle slices and apple chips, if desired.

ALL CRACKED UP

People crack up every time they see these cupcakes. First we paint the inside of plastic pull-apart Easter eggs with white chocolate to make the eggshells. Then we break a few and put them on top of mini cupcakes. To make sure everyone gets the yolk, we add a dollop of lemon curd. What a great idea for breakfast on April Fool's Day.

12 mini vanilla cupcakes baked in white paper liners

1 cup white candy melting wafers (Wilton)

2 teaspoons vegetable oil

1/2 cup prepared lemon curd

Yellow and red food coloring

1 cup canned vanilla frosting

7 plastic Easter eggs (3 1/2 inches long; see Sources)

1 clean egg carton (optional)

1. Place the white candy wafers in a microwavable bowl. Microwave for 10 seconds and stir. Repeat this process until the candies are melted and smooth, about 1 minute total.

2. Line a cookie sheet with wax paper and place in the refrigerator. Lightly oil a paper towel with the vegetable oil. Rub the inside of each plastic egg half with the oiled paper towel. Using your finger or a small brush, generously coat the inside of an oiled plastic egg half with the melted candy. Transfer the egg, open side down, to the cookie sheet in the refrigerator. Repeat with the remaining melted candy and plastic eggs. After a few minutes, check and touch up any eggs where the candy is too thin or there is a hole. Return to the refrigerator until set, about 5 minutes.

3. Remove the coated plastic eggs from the refrigerator and let stand for 1 minute. Carefully remove the hardened candy from the plastic eggs without breaking it (you will need 6 to 9 whole egg halves, plus any broken pieces for finishing).

4. Tint the lemon curd egg yolk yellow with 1 drop of red and 5 drops of yellow food coloring. Spoon the tinted lemon curd into a small ziplock bag, press out the excess air, and seal.

5. Spread the tops of the cupcakes with the vanilla frosting and smooth. Snip a small (1/8-inch) corner from the bag with the lemon curd. For the egg yolks, pipe a small mound of lemon curd on top of each of the frosted cupcakes. For the whole eggs, place the candy eggshells, open side down, on top of the lemon curd to cover. For the broken eggs, arrange broken pieces of shells around the yolk. Place the cupcakes in the clean egg carton if using.

CORN ON THE COB

Our corniest project ever! The ears are bursting with fresh summer flavor. But surprise: those kernels are jelly beans, the butter pats are fruit chews, and the salt and pepper is black and white sugar.

24 vanilla cupcakes baked in white paper liners

1 can (16 ounces) vanilla frosting

Yellow food coloring

About 3¹/₂ cups small jelly beans (Jelly Belly) in assorted yellow, cream, and white colors

4 pieces yellow fruit chews (Laffy Taffy, Starburst)

1 tablespoon each black and white decorating sugars (see Sources)

8 sets of corn holders (optional)

1. Tint the vanilla frosting pale yellow with the food coloring.

2. Working with 3 cupcakes at a time, spread yellow frosting on top of each. Arrange about 5 rows of jelly beans, close together, on each cupcake. Place the 3 cupcakes side by side on a corn dish or a serving platter. Repeat with the remaining cupcakes, frosting, and jelly beans.

3. Cut the fruit chews into eight 1-inch squares, and soften the edges slightly by hand so that they look melted. Place 1 square on top of each group of 3 cupcakes. Sprinkle with the sugars. Insert 1 corn holder, if using, in each of the end cupcakes.

SPAGHETTI AND MEATBALLS

ez
CUPCAKE

Drinking milk with spaghetti and meatballs might get you run out of your favorite Italian joint, but when your guests realize this is a platter of cupcakes with frosting pasta and strawberry sauce, everyone will want some. The chunk of Parmesan cheese in the background is actually white chocolate, and best of all, the meatballs are hazelnut chocolates right out of the bag.

10 **vanilla cupcakes baked in white paper liners**

 1 **can (16 ounces) vanilla frosting**

¹/₂ **teaspoon unsweetened cocoa powder**

 Yellow food coloring

11 **hazelnut chocolates (Ferrero Rocher), unwrapped**

³/₄ **cup low-sugar strawberry preserves (Smucker's; low-sugar has the best color)**

 2 **tablespoons grated white chocolate, plus an additional chunk for garnish**

1. Tint the vanilla frosting with the cocoa powder and 3 drops yellow food coloring and spread a thin layer on top of the cupcakes. Arrange the cupcakes on a serving platter so that they are touching.

2. Spoon the remaining frosting into a ziplock bag. Press out the excess air and seal the bag. Snip a ¹/₈-inch corner from the bag. Pipe the frosting all over the cupcakes to make the spaghetti, piling it high and allowing some of the spaghetti to hang over the edges.

3. Place the hazelnut chocolates and the strawberry preserves in a medium bowl and toss to coat. Spoon some of the preserves on top of the cupcakes. Place 1 hazelnut chocolate on each cupcake and 1 on the platter. Top the cupcakes

with the remaining strawberry preserves. Sprinkle with the grated white chocolate. Place the chunk of white chocolate on a separate plate with a small hand grater and bring to the table with the platter of spaghetti.

BAKE-SALE PIES

CUPCAKE

Our berry pie cupcakes are as easy as . . . pie! The blueberry and cherry filling is blue or red candies, and the frosting is tinted to look like a lattice crust. At your next bake sale, cover the table with these mini pastries, and we promise you will sell out!

24 vanilla cupcakes baked in silver foil liners (Reynolds)

2 cans (16 ounces each) vanilla frosting

Yellow food coloring

1 teaspoon unsweetened cocoa powder

1 cup each red and blue candy (My M&M's, Jelly Belly)

1. Tint the vanilla frosting with 3 or 4 drops of the yellow food coloring and the cocoa powder to make a light brown for the piecrust. Spread some of the frosting on top of a cupcake, leaving 1/4 inch of the cupcake edge exposed. For the filling, arrange about 25 like-colored candies close together on top of the cupcake. Repeat with the remaining cupcakes and like-colored candies.

2. Spoon the remaining light brown frosting into a ziplock bag, press out the excess air, and seal. Snip a small (1/8-inch) corner from the bag. For the lattice crust, pipe 4 or 5 lines across the top of a cupcake, about 1/2 inch apart. Pipe 4 or 5 more lines, on the diagonal. Pipe a beaded edge around the top of the cupcake (see page 13). Repeat with the remaining cupcakes and frosting.

3. Arrange the cupcakes on a wire rack and make several bake-sale tags to put with the cupcakes.

cherry pie

cherry
pie

BAKE
SALE

CHINESE TAKEOUT

House Special: Pork Lo Mein and Vegetarian Fried Rice. The kids will love this broccoli: green fruit chews with green frosting and nonpareils on a pile of lo mein noodles made of frosting squeezed from a ziplock bag. Serve fried rice on the side: puffed rice cereal tossed with fruit chews and jelly beans. And don't forget the caramel fortune cookies.

LO MEIN

6 **vanilla cupcakes baked in white paper liners**

6–8 **green fruit chews (Jolly Rancher, Laffy Taffy)**

3 **pink fruit chews (Jolly Rancher, Starburst, Laffy Taffy)**

1¹/₂ **cups canned vanilla frosting**

Green and yellow food coloring

1 **teaspoon unsweetened cocoa powder**

¹/₂ **cup dark green sprinkles (see Sources)**

1 **strand green licorice twist (Twizzlers Rainbow Twists), thinly sliced diagonally**

Large Chinese food take-out containers (optional; see Sources)

1. Line a cookie sheet with wax paper. For the broccoli stems, make a lengthwise slit halfway down the center of each green fruit chew and open slightly. Place the stems on the prepared cookie sheet. Microwave the pink fruit chews for 2 to 3 seconds to soften. Press the pink fruit chews together and roll out into a 2-by-3-inch rectangle about ¹/₈ inch thick. For the pork slivers, cut the flattened fruit chew rectangle crosswise into ¹/₈-inch-wide strips.

2. Tint ¹/₂ cup of the vanilla frosting bright green with the green food coloring, spoon the frosting into a ziplock bag, press out the excess air, and seal. Dissolve ¹/₂ teaspoon of the cocoa powder in 2 teaspoons of water and mix to make a smooth brown paste. Tint the remaining vanilla frosting light brown with 1 drop of yellow food coloring and the remaining ¹/₂ teaspoon cocoa powder.

Spread the darker brown paste down the side of a ziplock bag and then fill in with the light brown frosting. Press out the excess air and seal.

3. Place the green sprinkles in a small bowl. Snip a small (1/8-inch) corner from the bag with the green frosting. For the broccoli florets, pipe mounds of frosting on the tips of the split ends of the green fruit chews on the cookie sheet. Holding the broccoli by the stem, press the frosted end lightly into the sprinkles to cover completely; return to the cookie sheet (see the photo above).

4. Snip a small (1/8-inch) corner from the bag with the brown frosting. To make the lo mein noodles, pipe the frosting in an irregular pattern all over the cupcakes, piling it high and letting it hang over the edges (the darker brown frosting will look like soy sauce). Arrange the pink fruit chew pork slivers randomly on top of the cupcakes. Add one or two pieces of broccoli on top. For scallions, scatter a few green licorice slices on top of the cupcakes.

5. To get the full effect, carefully place the cupcakes in the Chinese take-out containers, if using.

FRIED RICE

6 vanilla cupcakes baked in white paper liners

2 tablespoons small light green jelly beans (Jelly Belly)

4 orange fruit chews (Tootsie Fruit Rolls)

3 yellow fruit chews (Tootsie Fruit Rolls, Starburst)

1¼ cups puffed rice cereal (Rice Krispies)

1¼ cups canned vanilla frosting

¼ teaspoon unsweetened cocoa powder

2 strands green licorice twists (Twizzlers Rainbow Twists), thinly sliced diagonally

2 tablespoons chocolate sauce (optional)

1. For the peas, cut the green jelly beans in half crosswise with a small knife or clean scissors. For the carrots, cut the orange fruit chews into ¼-inch cubes. For the scrambled egg, cut the yellow fruit chews into small strips and pinch to soften the sharp edges. For the rice, place the rice cereal in a medium bowl.

2. Tint the vanilla frosting pale beige with the cocoa powder. Spread the tops of the cupcakes with a thin layer of frosting; use about ½ cup of the frosting. Heat the remaining ¾ cup frosting in a small microwavable bowl in the microwave until it has the texture of lightly whipped cream, about 15 seconds. Pour the heated frosting over the cereal, tossing to coat evenly. Reserve a few of the cut jelly beans and fruit chews for finishing and toss the rest with the cereal mixture. Spoon about ¼ cup of the cereal mixture on top of each frosted cupcake, pressing down to secure. Arrange the reserved candy pieces on top of the cupcakes. For the scallions, scatter a few licorice pieces on top.

3. Carefully place the cupcakes in large Chinese take-out containers, if using.

4. For the soy sauce, pour the chocolate sauce into a small dish, if desired.

FORTUNE COOKIES

24 mini chocolate cupcakes baked in white paper liners

1 can (16 ounces) vanilla frosting

48 caramels (Kraft), unwrapped

24 $^3/_8$-by-2$^1/_2$-inch slips of paper with printed fortunes (make your own on a computer or write them by hand and cut them to size)

Orange candy fruit slices (optional)

1. Spread the tops of the cupcakes with the vanilla frosting and smooth.

2. For the cookies, microwave several caramels at a time for 2 to 3 seconds to soften slightly. Press 2 caramels together and roll out to an approximately 3-inch round. Cut out a 3-inch circle using clean scissors, a cookie cutter, or the rim of a glass. Repeat with the remaining caramels. Place a paper message down the center of a caramel circle, allowing it to overhang one side. Fold the opposite sides of the caramel circle up over the message and bring the two sides together at the top edge to create a half-moon shape that is open in the center like a taco shell. Pull the two folded ends down and together to make a fortune-cookie shape.

3. Place the caramel fortune cookies on top of the cupcakes, pressing down lightly to adhere and place the orange candy fruit slices on the side, if using.

BANANA SPLIT

The inside scoop on this split is that anisette cookies dipped in melted yellow frosting and placed end to end make the banana. The ice cream is frosting tinted to look like vanilla, strawberry, and chocolate. The cherries are shaped from red fruit chews and have licorice lace for stems.

12 vanilla cupcakes baked in white paper liners

1 can (16 ounces) plus 1 cup vanilla frosting

3 tablespoons low-sugar strawberry preserves (Smucker's)

1 cup canned chocolate frosting

Yellow food coloring

8 anisette cookies (Stella D'oro Anisette Toast)

1 red licorice lace

12 red fruit chews (Jolly Rancher, Starburst)

12 thin pretzel sticks (Bachman)

1/2 cup hot fudge sauce, plus extra for serving

1 cup whipped topping (Cool Whip)

Coarse white decorating sugar for sundae dish (see Sources)

2 tablespoons chocolate sprinkles

1. Divide the can of vanilla frosting evenly between two bowls. Mix the strawberry preserves into one bowl of frosting until well blended. Spoon the chocolate frosting into another bowl. Freeze all three bowls of frosting until firm, about 30 minutes. Tint the remaining 1 cup vanilla frosting pale yellow with the yellow food coloring. Spoon the yellow frosting into a microwavable measuring cup.

2. Place a wire rack over a cookie sheet. Microwave the yellow frosting, stopping to stir frequently, until it has the texture of lightly whipped cream, 30 to 35 seconds. Dip an anisette cookie into the melted frosting, tipping the measuring

cup to cover the cookie almost completely. Pull the cookie out of the frosting and allow the excess frosting to drain back into the cup. Place the dipped cookie on the wire rack, flat side down. Repeat with the remaining cookies. Refrigerate until set, about 20 minutes.

3. For the cherry stems, cut the red licorice lace into six 2-inch pieces. Cut each piece in half lengthwise. For the cherries, microwave several red fruit chews for 2 to 3 seconds. Shape each fruit chew into a ball. Use a toothpick to score one side of the fruit chew to shape the cherry and to make a hole in the top. Repeat with the remaining fruit chews. Insert a pretzel stick into the base of each cherry for support (see page 19). Insert a piece of trimmed licorice into the hole on the top of the cherry. Spoon the fudge sauce into a ziplock bag. Spoon the whipped topping into a ziplock bag. Press out the excess air and seal the bags. Refrigerate the whipped topping until ready to serve.

4. For the vanilla ice cream, scoop the chilled vanilla frosting into small pieces, using an ice cream scoop or a large spoon. Place the frosting pieces, overlapping slightly, on top of 4 of the cupcakes to look like a scoop of ice cream. Repeat with the chocolate and the strawberry frostings on top of the remaining 8 cupcakes.

5. Sprinkle four sundae dishes with the white decorating sugar, if desired. Arrange 3 cupcakes, one of each flavor, in each sundae dish. When ready to serve, snip a $1/4$-inch corner from the bag with the fudge sauce and pipe a small amount on top of the vanilla scoop. Snip a $1/2$-inch corner from the bag with the whipped topping and pipe a dollop of whipped topping on top of each scoop. Sprinkle the tops with the chocolate sprinkles. Insert the cherry candies, pretzel stem down and licorice lace up, into the scoops. Arrange 2 dipped anisette cookies behind the scoops in each dish to make the banana. Serve with extra fudge sauce.

Happy Birthday, Cupcake!

Let's make it all about you. Whether it's bling, karaoke, painting, or crocs, celebrating fixations makes a birthday that rocks. Robots, race cars, fuzzy monsters too. Go ahead, enjoy, it's all a part of you. Indulge your passions, fuel a fire, transform that obsession into the cupcake of your desire.

Ring Bling   54

Fur Balls and String Monsters   57

Formula One Cupcakes   60

Flower Power   65

Karaoke Cupcakes   68

Slumber Party   70

Artist's Palette   74

Robocup   76

Jungle Fever   79

Ring Pop candy

Chiclets

decorating sugar

vanilla frosting

foil liner

colored paper

ring pop base

RING BLING

Mini cupcake jewelry made from Ring Pops will turn your little girl's party into the one not to miss. Set up gem stations where kids can choose from their favorite candies and sparkling sugars to create their own Ring Bling cupcakes. For even bigger bling, try the finger plate variation that can hold a whopping 24 carats of candy.

24 mini vanilla cupcakes baked in gold or silver liners (see Sources)

24 Ring Pops or 24 Fingerfood party plates for the ring bases (see Sources)

Colored decorating sugars (see Sources)

1 can (16 ounces) plus 1 cup vanilla frosting

Assorted candies (M&M's Minis, Chiclets Tiny Size gum, Jujubes, Tootsie Pop Drops, and spice drops, if using Fingerfood party plates)

3/4 cup white chocolate chips

Colored paper, cut into 3-inch scalloped circles (Marvy paper punch; see Sources)

1. If using Ring Pops for the base, remove the hard candies from the rings; set aside. Cut a small hole in the center of the colored paper circles and insert the plastic tip of the ring through the paper. Use a toothpick to poke a hole in the base of the cupcake liners.

2. Place each colored sugar into a small shallow bowl. Spread the tops of the mini cupcakes with the vanilla frosting and smooth. Arrange candies on top as desired to make the ring design, leaving the center open for the large gemstone from the Ring Pop. Roll the top of the cupcake in the desired colored sugar. Press the Ring Pop gemstone into the center of the cupcake. Repeat with the remaining cupcakes, candies, and sugars.

3. Place the white chocolate chips in a ziplock bag; do not seal. Microwave for about 10 seconds to soften. Massage the mixture and return to the microwave. Repeat the process until the chocolate is smooth, about 1 minute total (see page 18). Press out the excess air. Snip a small ($\frac{1}{8}$-inch) corner from the bag. Pipe a dot of melted white chocolate on the plastic tip of each ring before adding the cupcake. Use a small juice glass to hold the Ring Pop ring upright and refrigerate until set, about 5 minutes.

4. If using Fingerfood party plates, roll out a few spice drops on a lightly sugared work surface to a $\frac{1}{8}$-inch thickness. Cut into small shapes using scissors or small cookie cutters; set aside. Place each colored sugar into a small shallow bowl. Spread the top of a mini cupcake with the vanilla frosting and smooth. Arrange candies and some of the cut spice drops on top of the cupcake as the ring design. Roll the top of the cupcake in the desired colored sugar. Repeat with the remaining cupcakes, candies, and sugars.

5. Spoon the remaining vanilla frosting into a ziplock bag, press out the excess air, and seal. Snip a small ($\frac{1}{8}$-inch) corner from the bag and pipe lines and dots of frosting along the outer edge of the plates, adding sugar or remaining candies as desired (leave the center of the plate open for the cupcake).

6. Place the white chocolate chips in a ziplock bag; do not seal. Microwave for about 10 seconds to soften. Massage the mixture and return to the microwave. Repeat the process until the chocolate is smooth, about 1 minute total (see page 18). Press out the excess air. Snip a small ($\frac{1}{8}$-inch) corner from the bag and pipe a dot of chocolate in the center of the Fingerfood plate. Place the bottom of the decorated cupcake into the chocolate, pressing to secure. Use a small juice glass to hold the Fingerfood plate upright and refrigerate until set, about 5 minutes.

FUR BALLS AND STRING MONSTERS

ez
CUPCAKE

It was a mosh, yes, a monster mosh. It was so simple, we were done in a flash. We used a Dum Dum, a sour fruit ring, M&M eyes, and a mini cupcake thing. Frosting turned green, orange, purple too. We created a monster, so frightening and new. Go grab some candy, a cupcake or two, and in no time at all, you'll be doing it too.

12 **vanilla cupcakes baked in orange, green, and purple paper liners (see Sources)**

12 **mini vanilla cupcakes, paper liners removed**

1 **can (16 ounces) vanilla frosting**

Green, orange, and purple food coloring (use neon food coloring for brighter colors; McCormick)

24 **mini lollipops (Dum Dums), unwrapped**

24 **peach or green apple gummy rings (O's)**

24 **brown mini candy-coated chocolates (M&M's Minis)**

12 **assorted color candy-coated chocolates (M&M's Minis)**

1. Spoon 2 tablespoons vanilla frosting into a small zi-plock bag. Divide the remaining vanilla frosting among three bowls and tint each a different color with the food coloring. Spoon each color of frosting into a separate ziplock bag, press out the excess air, and seal the bags.

2. Insert a lollipop stick through a gummy ring, pushing it through the candy from the center to outer edge. Bring the gummy ring up around the lollypop, like a bonnet, to make the eyes. Continue with the remaining gummy rings and lollipops.

3. Snip a small (¹/₈-inch) corner from the bags with the frostings. Pipe a dot of tinted frosting on top of the standard cupcakes. Place a mini cupcake on top, flat side down. Starting at the edge of the standard cupcake and using the tinted frosting, pipe fur with a squeeze-release-pull action (see page 13). Continue until the entire exposed cupcake assembly is covered. Repeat with the remaining cupcakes and colored frosting.

4. Insert 2 like-colored lollipop eyes into the top of each cupcake assembly. Pipe a dot of vanilla frosting in the center of each lollipop and add a brown candy for the pupil. Add a colored candy to the top of the frosting for the nose. Repeat with the remaining lollipop eyes and cupcakes.

VARIATION: String monsters: Follow steps 1 and 2. Snip a small (¹/₈-inch) corner from the bags with the frosting. Pipe a dot of tinted frosting on top of the standard cupcakes. Place a mini cupcake on top, flat side down. Pipe the tinted frosting all over the cupcakes to make the string, making sure to cover cupcakes completely. Continue with step 4.

FORMULA ONE CUPCAKES

Preheat your ovens, and sort your candies. Our Formula One race car has oversize doughnut tires, a chocolate spoiler and straight pipes, and a shiny red-sugar-coated paint job. Drivers, start your engines!

19 vanilla cupcakes baked in red paper liners (see Sources)

1 can (16 ounces) plus 1 cup vanilla frosting

Red and black food coloring (see Sources)

1 cup canned dark chocolate frosting

1 cup dark cocoa candy melting wafers (Wilton)

2 vanilla wafers

1 thin pretzel stick (Bachman)

1 graham cracker

1 cup red decorating sugar (see Sources)

2 yellow and 4 white candies (Mentos)

2 chocolate-frosted doughnuts

2 mini chocolate-frosted doughnuts

2 chocolate sticks (Hershey's or Kit Kat)

1. Spoon ¼ cup vanilla frosting into a ziplock bag, press out the excess air, seal, and set aside. Tint the remaining vanilla frosting red with the red food coloring, cover, and set aside. Tint the dark chocolate frosting black with the black food coloring. Spoon the black frosting into a ziplock bag, press out the air, seal, and set aside.

2. Place the dark cocoa candy melting wafers in a ziplock bag; do not seal. Microwave for 10 seconds, massage the bag, and repeat the process until smooth, about 45 seconds total (see page 18). Press out the excess air and seal. Place the templates (pages 63 and 64) on a cookie sheet and cover with wax paper. Snip a small (⅛-inch) corner from the bag and pipe the outline of the spoiler and

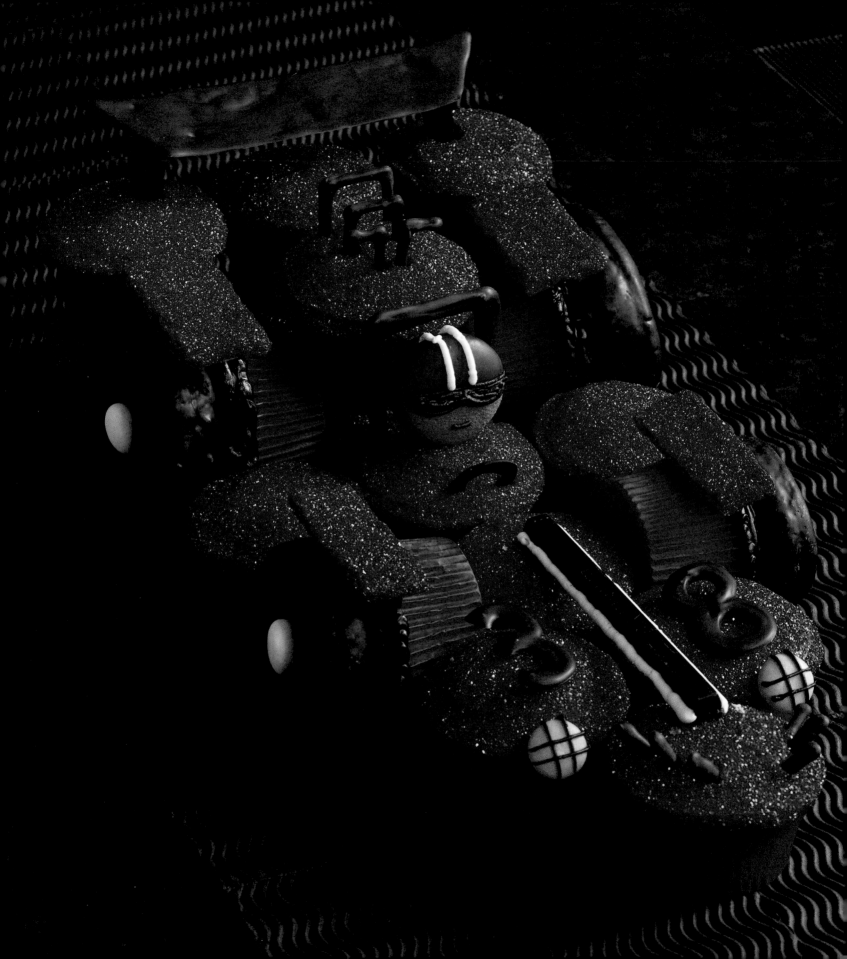

racing numbers, then fill in with the melted candy. Tap the pan lightly to smooth the surface. Repeat, using the templates, to make the roll bar, straight pipes, steering wheel, and exhaust pipe parts. Refrigerate until set, about 5 minutes.

3. Pipe a dot of the melted candy onto the flat side of 1 vanilla wafer. Place the end of the pretzel stick into the melted candy to cover (see page 19). To make the driver's head, sandwich the remaining vanilla wafer, flat side down, on top, pressing into the melted candy. Place on the cookie sheet and refrigerate until set, about 5 minutes.

4. Cut the graham cracker with a serrated knife crosswise into 4 equal pieces. Trim $1/4$ inch lengthwise from 2 of the pieces. Place the red sugar in a small bowl. Spread a very thin layer of the red frosting on top of the graham cracker pieces. Invert the pieces into the red sugar and press lightly to coat. Transfer the pieces, sugar side up, to a cookie sheet.

5. Reserve $1/3$ cup of the red frosting in a small bowl. Spread the remaining red frosting on top of 15 of the cupcakes and smooth. Starting on the edge, roll the cupcakes in the red sugar to cover completely (see page 17).

6. Heat the reserved $1/3$ cup red frosting in the microwave for about 5 seconds, stir well, and heat again to get the consistency of slightly whipped cream. Dip one side of the cookie head into the frosting to cover. Dip the other side halfway into the frosting to make the top of the helmet. Allow the excess frosting to drip off back into the bowl (see page 15). Transfer to a wax paper–lined cookie sheet, half-dipped side up. Refrigerate for 15 minutes.

7. Snip a very small ($1/16$-inch) corner from the bags with the vanilla and black frosting. Pipe the mouth and goggles on the racer's face with the black frosting. Pipe a dot of black frosting on one edge of 2 red-sugared cupcakes. Attach a yellow candy to each frosting dot as the headlight. Pipe crosshatch lines on the yellow candies with the black frosting to make the light guards. Snip a larger opening from the bag with the black frosting and pipe frosting on top of the 4 unfrosted cupcakes. Spread the frosting to the edge and smooth. For the front and rear tires, press a chocolate doughnut, flat side down, on top of each of the 4 cupcakes.

8. Arrange the cupcakes on a serving platter or cutting board in the shape of the race car (see the photo on page 61): 1 red cupcake in front, a row of the 2 red

cupcakes with the headlights, a row of 3 made up of the 2 mini-doughnut cupcakes on their sides as the front wheels and 1 red cupcake in the center, a row
of 3 red cupcakes, a row of 3 made up of the 2 doughnut cupcakes on their
sides as the rear wheels with 1 red cupcake in the center and the center cupcake topped with another red cupcake, and a last row of 3 red cupcakes with
another row of 3 red cupcakes on top.

9. Cut one of the chocolate sticks in half crosswise. Insert each cut piece of chocolate into the outer cupcakes in the last row. Pipe a dot of black frosting on the
end of each chocolate stick. Carefully peel the chocolate spoiler from the wax
paper and attach to the chocolate sticks, with the longer side facing out. Pipe a
decorative edge around the wheels with the black frosting to fill the gap at the
cupcake and attach the sugared graham cracker pieces to the frosting to make
fenders; put the larger pieces on top of the larger doughnuts. Pipe 2 white lines

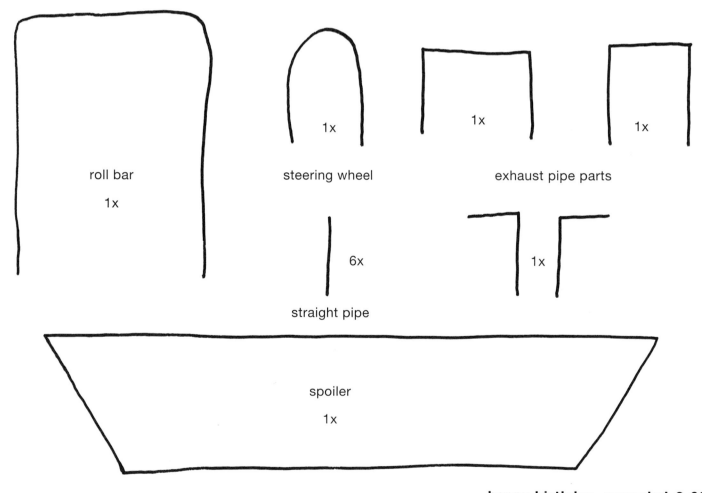

roll bar

1x

steering wheel

1x

exhaust pipe parts

1x

6x

straight pipe

1x

spoiler

1x

of frosting on top of the helmet and insert the head, pretzel stick down, into the center cupcake as the driver. Place the remaining chocolate stick down the center front of the car and pipe a white line down either side of the chocolate stick using the vanilla frosting. Carefully peel the numbers, roll bar, straight pipes, steering wheel, and exhaust pipe parts from the wax paper and place on the cupcakes as shown in the photograph. Pipe black frosting into the opening of each doughnut wheel and add the white candies as the hubcaps.

38

FLOWER POWER

Please *do* eat the daisies—and the daffodils and posies too. Each blossom in our garden of candy delights is built on a cookie, with melted white chocolate holding the petals in place. Pretzel supports keep our garden standing tall (see the photo on page 3).

  6 **vanilla cupcakes baked in green paper liners (see Sources)**

1/4 **cup yellow decorating sugar (see Sources)**

  3 **tablespoons pink or light pink decorating sugar (see Sources)**

  3 **marshmallows**

20 **mini marshmallows**

  2 **thin chocolate cookies (Famous Chocolate Wafers)**

  7 **vanilla wafers**

  5 **mini vanilla wafers**

1/2 **cup white chocolate chips**

  6 **orange candies (Runts)**

30–33 **small red jelly beans (Jelly Belly)**

  3 **yellow cereal O's (Froot Loops)**

  4 **spice drops (orange, red, and yellow)**

25 **orange candy-coated chocolates (M&M's)**

  5 **green mini candy-coated chocolates (M&M's Minis)**

24 **thin pretzel sticks (Bachman)**

  5 **candy spearmint leaves (Farley's)**

  1 **cup flaked sweetened coconut**

    Yellow and green food coloring

  1 **cup canned vanilla frosting**

  1 **cup small green jelly beans (Jelly Belly; optional)**

1. Place the yellow and pink decorating sugars in separate small shallow bowls. Using scissors, cut the standard marshmallows crosswise into 5 pieces, allowing the pieces to fall into the yellow sugar. Shake the bowl, tossing the marshmallow pieces to coat with the sugar. Cut the mini marshmallows on the diagonal and let them fall into the pink sugar bowl. Toss the pieces with the sugar until coated.

2. Arrange like cookies close together on a large cookie sheet. Place the white chocolate chips in a ziplock bag. Do not seal the bag. Microwave for 10 seconds to soften. Massage the chips in the bag, return to the microwave, and repeat the process until the chocolate is smooth, about 1 minute total (see page 18). Press out the excess air and seal.

3. Snip a very small ($1/16$-inch) corner from the bag with the chocolate. For the yellow flowers, pipe a circle of melted chocolate $1/2$ inch from the edge of the chocolate wafers and another small circle in the center. Add the yellow sugared marshmallow pieces, overlapping them slightly along the outer edge, and 3 orange candies in the center. For the red flowers, pipe white chocolate in a circle along the edge of 3 of the standard vanilla wafers. Attach the red jelly beans along the edge, side by side and radiating out from the center. Pipe a dot of white chocolate in the center and add a yellow cereal O. For the pink flowers, pipe white chocolate in a circle along the edge of the 4 remaining standard vanilla wafers. Attach the pink sugared marshmallows side by side, pointed ends radiating out. Flatten the spice drops slightly. Pipe a dot of white chocolate in the center of the vanilla

wafers and add a spice drop. For the orange flowers, pipe some white chocolate on the flat side of the mini vanilla wafers. Arrange 5 orange candy-coated chocolates on top, close to the edge. Add the mini green candies in the center. Place all of the cookie flowers in the refrigerator until set, about 5 minutes.

4. Remove the cookie flowers from the refrigerator and turn over. Pipe a line of white chocolate on the center of each cookie, reheating the chocolate in the microwave for several seconds to soften if necessary. Place the end of a pretzel stick into the chocolate on each cookie and turn to coat (see page 19). Refrigerate until set, about 5 minutes.

5. Place the spearmint leaves flat side down. Cut the leaves in half horizontally so they are thin. Insert a pretzel stick into the wide end to make 10 leaves.

6. Place the coconut in a ziplock bag. Add a few drops of yellow and 1 drop of green food coloring. Massage the bag with the coconut until completely tinted (see page 16). Pour the coconut into a shallow bowl. Tint the vanilla frosting light green with the green and yellow food coloring. Spread the green frosting on top of the cupcakes and smooth. Roll the edges of the cupcakes in the coconut (see page 17).

7. Arrange the cupcakes close together in a shallow dish. Sprinkle some of the green jelly beans in the open areas. Just before serving, insert the pretzel ends of the flowers into the cupcakes, trimming the pretzel sticks as necessary to make a full bouquet. Add the spearmint leaves.

KARAOKE CUPCAKES

These cupcakes will inspire your inner idol with miniature microphones made from an ice cream cone and a doughnut hole coated with silver sprinkles. There's a licorice remote antenna at the base of the cone, so rock out and conquer the stage.

24 vanilla cupcakes baked in silver foil liners (Reynolds)

1 can (16 ounces) plus 1 cup vanilla frosting
Red food coloring

24 mini ice cream cones (Joy Kids Cones)

24 pieces pink licorice pastels (Jelly Belly)

24 plain doughnut holes

1 cup mini silver dragées (see Sources) or decorating sugar or sprinkles

1. Tint the can of vanilla frosting light pink with a few drops of red food coloring. Cover and set aside. Spoon ¼ cup of the remaining frosting into a small ziplock bag, press out the air, seal, and set aside.

2. For the antenna, use a wooden skewer or toothpick to make a small hole in the base of each cone. Snip a small (⅛-inch) corner from the bag with the vanilla frosting and pipe a small dot of frosting into the hole. Insert a pink licorice pastel halfway into each hole. Pipe a line of vanilla frosting around the top inside edge of each cone. Press a doughnut hole into the opening of the cone.

3. Place the silver dragées (or decorating sugar or sprinkles) in a small bowl. Gently spread a thin layer of the remaining ¾ cup vanilla frosting over a doughnut hole. Press the frosting into the dragées to cover the doughnut hole completely. Repeat with the remaining doughnut holes.

4. Spread the tops of the cupcakes with the pink frosting and smooth. Place the cone microphones on top of the cupcakes, pressing down to secure.

SLUMBER PARTY

A slumber party is a dream for the kids but can be a nightmare for the
parents. The drowsy tots on board these cupcakes may be the only
ones sleeping, so serve with glasses of warm milk to ease the party into
dreamland.

6 vanilla cupcakes baked in white paper liners

1 can (16 ounces) vanilla frosting

   Orange, yellow, and green food coloring (see Sources)

1/2 cup chocolate frosting

6 marshmallows

2 small pink jelly beans (Jelly Belly)

2 each light pink, dark pink, yellow, orange, blue, purple, and
   green fruit chews (Starburst, Laffy Taffy, Airheads)

6 mini vanilla wafers

   Pink and red heart decors

2 bear-shaped graham crackers (Teddy Grahams)

   Red sprinkles

1. Spoon 2 tablespoons of the vanilla frosting into a small ziplock bag, press out
   the excess air, and seal. Tint 2 tablespoons of the vanilla frosting each with the
   orange, yellow, and green food coloring and spoon into separate small ziplock
   bags. Press out the excess air and seal the bags. Place the chocolate frosting in
   a ziplock bag, press out the excess air, and seal.

2. Spread the tops of the cupcakes with the remaining 1 1/2 cups vanilla frosting
   and smooth. Cut the marshmallows in half lengthwise. Place 1 marshmallow
   piece, lengthwise and cut side down, on the lower half of one of the cupcakes.
   Place another marshmallow piece crosswise, cut side down, near the top edge

of the cupcake to make the pillow. Repeat with the remaining 5 cupcakes. On one of the cupcakes, press the jelly beans into the frosting at the bottom edge, just below the end of the marshmallow, to make the feet.

3. Working with 2 like-colored fruit chews at a time, heat them in the microwave for 2 to 3 seconds to soften. Press the fruit chews together and roll out on a sheet of wax paper to $1/16$ inch thick. Cut a 2-inch square from all but the purple fruit-chew piece and a 2-by-$1/2$-inch strip from the scraps. Using craft scissors with a decorative edge, cut along one side of each strip to make a zigzag blanket edge. Press contrasting colors of fruit-chew squares and strips together to make the blankets with borders. Cut a $3/4$-by-$1^1/2$-inch rectangle from the rolled-out purple fruit-chew piece. Cut a $3/4$-inch square from the scraps of the yellow fruit chews and place on one side of the purple fruit chew. Fold the purple fruit chew over the yellow to make a book.

4. Snip a $1/16$-inch corner from each of the 5 bags with the frostings. Pipe a dot of frosting on the marshmallow pillow and add the vanilla wafer, flat side down. Using the orange, yellow, or chocolate frosting, pipe hair along the top edge of each wafer. Pipe the children's eyelids or eyebrows with chocolate frosting and the eyes with a dot of vanilla frosting, then a dot of chocolate. Pipe a dot of vanilla frosting for the mouths and add the pink or red heart decors. Pipe the teddy bear's eyes and mouth with chocolate frosting. Pipe a tiny dot of vanilla

frosting for the bear's nose and add a red sprinkle. On the cover of the book, pipe a ghost with vanilla frosting and writing with chocolate frosting.

5. Press the blankets over the marshmallow bodies and pipe decorations on top with the colored frosting. Attach the teddy bears and the book with dots of frosting.

ARTIST'S PALETTE

CUPCAKE

What's our favorite canvas? Cupcakes, of course! Tint frosting to make the paint colors and sculpt a brush from Tootsie Rolls and a bread stick.

7 vanilla cupcakes, 1 in each of the following paper liners: yellow, orange, red, pink, purple, blue, and green (see Sources)

3 chocolate chews (Tootsie Rolls)

1 can (16 ounces) vanilla frosting

1 plain bread stick, 6 inches long

1 3-inch piece strawberry fruit leather (Fruit by the Foot)

Yellow, orange, red, purple, blue, and green food coloring

Painter's palette (optional; can be cut from a piece of cardboard or found at arts and crafts stores; see Sources)

1. For the bristles of the paintbrush, microwave the chocolate chews for no more than 3 seconds on high. Press the candies together and roll out on a clean work surface into a $1/8$-inch-thick rectangle about $2^{1/2}$ by 4 inches. Use scissors to cut the rectangle crosswise, almost all the way through, every scant 1/8 inch; it will look like fringe. Place a dot of frosting $1/2$ inch from one end of the bread stick. Place the uncut side of the rolled-out chocolate chew against the frosted end of the bread stick and roll it around the bread stick to make the brush. Place the fruit leather overlapping the chocolate and the bread stick and roll it around the bread stick, ending with a dot of water to secure. Loosen the chocolate fringe and lightly press the ends together to make a paintbrush; set aside.

2. Divide the frosting evenly among seven small bowls. Make sure to keep the bowls covered with plastic wrap to prevent the tops from drying. Tint each bowl of frosting a different color with the food colors. (Use the red food coloring to make one bowl of red frosting and one bowl of pink.)

3. Matching the frosting color to the color of the paper liners, spread an even layer of frosting over the cupcakes. Arrange the cupcakes on a painter's palette, if desired, and add the paintbrush.

ROBOCUP

Under that shiny sci-fi veneer lies a tasty cyborg: half robot, all cupcake. Add a few gizmos and blinking lights made from colorful candies and frosting, and your Robocup is ready to roll.

18 vanilla cupcakes baked in silver foil liners (Reynolds)

1 can (16 ounces) plus 1 cup vanilla frosting
  Black food coloring (see Sources)

5 whole graham crackers

1 cup gray decorating sugar (see Sources)

4 plain bread sticks

4 thin wheat sticks (Pringles)

3 red and 4 white jelly rings (Chuckles)

2 vanilla wafers

1 tube (4.25 ounces) brown decorating icing (Cake Mate)

16 brown, 6 blue, 4 green, 4 yellow, and 2 orange mini candy-coated chocolates (M&M's Minis)

6 red, 2 blue, and 2 brown candy-coated chocolates (M&M's)

5 red and 1 white licorice pastels (Jelly Belly)

1 square candy-coated gum (Chiclets)

1 red gumdrop (Dots)

1. Tint all of the vanilla frosting light gray with a few drops of the black food coloring. Spoon ³/₄ cup of the frosting into a ziplock bag, press out the air, seal, and set aside. Cover the remaining frosting with plastic wrap until ready to use.

2. For the head, using a serrated knife, trim 1 inch from one end of 1 whole graham cracker, reserving the trimmed piece for the mouth. Cut the remaining 4 whole graham crackers in half crosswise to make 8 square pieces. Set aside 4 squares for the chest. For the legs, cut 1 square in half to make 2 rectangles. For the arms and feet, cut 2 squares in half on a diagonal to make pieces that are 1 inch

wide at the top and 1¼ inches wide at the bottom. For the pelvis, trim ¾ inch from 2 corners of 1 square. Put the sugar in a small shallow bowl.

3. Spread a very thin layer of the gray frosting on top of each graham cracker and smooth. Place a frosted cracker piece, frosted side down, into the sugar to cover. Transfer the sugar-coated cracker piece to a cookie sheet, sugared side up. Repeat with the remaining crackers and sugar.

4. Using a serrated knife, cut the plain bread sticks into four 2½-inch pieces. Cut the thin wheat sticks into three 3-inch pieces and four 1-inch pieces. For the hands, remove one fourth of 2 red jelly rings. Press together the red jelly ring pieces and the remaining red jelly ring and roll out on a lightly sugared work surface to a ⅛-inch thickness. To make the red control panel, use scissors to cut the sheet of rolled candy into a 1-by-2½-inch oval. Roll out 2 of the white jelly rings on a lightly sugared surface to a ⅛-inch thickness. For the semicircular meter panel, cut a 2½-inch circle from the flattened jelly rings. Cut a 1¼-inch hole in the center and cut the ring in half. Using the scraps, cut a 1½-by-1-inch rectangle for the mouth.

5. Spread the remaining gray frosting on top of the cupcakes and smooth. Arrange the cupcakes on a serving platter in this order: 3 across for the head, leaving space between the head and chest, a square group of 4 for the chest, 2 lengthwise for each arm, leaving a space between the hands and the chest, 1 for the pelvis, and 3 lengthwise for each leg.

6. Snip a small (⅛-inch) corner from the bag with the gray frosting. Using the photo as a guide, arrange the sugared graham crackers, bread sticks, and vanilla wafers on top of the cupcakes, securing with dots of gray frosting. Make sure that the chest crackers line up evenly. Pipe beaded lines (see page 13) of gray frosting along the seams between the chest crackers. Add additional beaded lines to crackers and bread sticks.

7. Pipe dots of frosting and attach the 2 remaining white jelly rings to make the ears, the two trimmed red jelly rings for the hands, and the jelly shapes cut for the control panel, meter panel, and mouth. Using the brown icing, pipe lines on top of the meter panel. Using dots of gray frosting, attach the wheat sticks as the 4 hand extensions and 3 antennae, M&M's as the bolts, eyes, buttons, lights, and toes, licorice pastels as the mouth grill and nose, gum as the start button, and gumdrop as the antenna light.

JUNGLE FEVER

If those crocs and hippos get a taste of flamingo, they are in for a real treat, because the flavor is a subtle mix of pink jelly bean, banana Runt, pink chocolate, and pretzel. The crocs and hippos don't taste bad either, since they are made from Nutter Butter cookies and Froot Loops.

HIPPOS

4 **vanilla cupcakes baked in blue paper liners (see Sources)**

^{1}/$_3$ **cup blue decorating sugar (see Sources)**

1 **cup canned vanilla frosting**

Neon blue food coloring (McCormick)

4 **peanut butter sandwich cookies (Nutter Butter)**

8 **mini chocolate chips**

16 **pieces orange cereal O's (Froot Loops)**

1. Place the blue sugar in a small shallow bowl.

2. Spoon 2 tablespoons of the vanilla frosting into a small ziplock bag, press out the excess air, seal, and set aside. Tint the remaining vanilla frosting blue with the food coloring. Spread the blue frosting on top of the cupcakes and smooth. Roll the edge of the cupcakes in the sugar (see page 17).

3. For the hippo heads, press a cookie into the frosting of each cupcake, allowing one third of the cookie to hang over the edge. Snip a small (^{1}/$_8$-inch) corner from the bag with the vanilla frosting. Pipe dots of the frosting onto the peanut butter cookie for the eyes, nostrils, and ears. Attach the chocolate chips, flat side up, to the frosting to make the eyes and attach the cereal pieces to make the ears and nose.

FLAMINGOS

12 mini vanilla cupcakes baked in white paper liners

1 cup pink candy melting wafers (Wilton)

12 thin pretzel sticks (Bachman)

12 large pink jelly beans (Farley's)

6 banana-shaped candies (Runts), halved crosswise

1/2 cup pink decorating sugar (see Sources)

1 cup canned vanilla frosting

Black food coloring (see Sources)

1. Line a cookie sheet with wax paper. Place the pink candy melting wafers in a 1-cup glass measuring cup. Microwave for 10 seconds to soften, stir, return to the microwave, and repeat until the candy is smooth, about 1 minute total.

2. For the necks and heads, hold the end of a pretzel stick and tip the measuring cup; dip the stick into the melted candy to cover almost completely. Allow the excess candy to drip off back into the cup. Transfer the coated pretzel stick to the wax paper. Dip one end of a jelly bean into the melted candy and attach to the coated end of the pretzel at an angle to make the head. Repeat with the remaining pretzels and jelly beans. For the beaks, dip the cut ends of the halved banana candies into the melted candy. Attach to the other end of the jelly bean to make the beak (see the photo above). Refrigerate until set, about 5 minutes.

3. Spoon the remaining melted candy into a small ziplock bag; do not seal the bag. Reheat in the microwave for 5 to 10 seconds if necessary. Press out the excess air and seal. Place the wing templates (page 81) on a cookie sheet and cover with wax paper. Snip a small ($^1/_8$-inch) corner from the bag and pipe the outline of the wings, then fill in with melted candy. Tap the pan lightly to smooth surface. Repeat to make 12 sets of wings. Refrigerate until set, about 5 minutes.

4. Place the pink sugar in a small shallow bowl. Tint 1 tablespoon of the vanilla frosting black with the food coloring. Spoon into a ziplock bag, press out the excess air, seal, and set aside. Spread the remaining vanilla frosting on top of the mini cupcakes, mounding it slightly in the center. Starting on the edge, roll the cupcakes in the pink sugar to cover completely (see page 17).

5. Gently peel the chilled flamingo head assemblies and wings from the wax paper. Insert the pretzel stick all the way into each cupcake close to one side. Press the wings into each cupcake on either side of the neck. Snip a very small ($^1/_{16}$-inch) corner from the bag with the black frosting and pipe dots of frosting for the eyes and a line on the banana candy to mark the tip of the beak.

CROCODILES

4 **vanilla cupcakes baked in blue paper liners (see Sources)**

1 **cup canned vanilla frosting**

Black and neon blue food coloring (McCormick, or see Sources)

$^1/_3$ **cup each blue and green decorating sugar (see Sources)**

4 **peanut butter sandwich cookies (Nutter Butter)**

8 **pieces green cereal O's (Froot Loops)**

1. Tint 2 tablespoons of the vanilla frosting black with the food coloring. Spoon the black frosting into a ziplock bag, press out the excess air, seal, and set aside. Spoon $^1/_4$ cup of the vanilla frosting into a ziplock bag, press out the excess air, seal, and set aside. Tint the remaining vanilla frosting blue with the food coloring.

2. Place the blue sugar in a small shallow bowl. Spread the blue frosting on top of the cupcakes. Roll the edge of the cupcakes in the sugar (see page 17).

3. For the croc heads, trim the edges of the cookies with a serrated knife to form a long V-shape. Place the green sugar in a shallow bowl. Snip a small (1/8-inch) corner from the bag with the vanilla frosting and pipe on top of the trimmed cookies to cover; spread smooth. Press the frosted side of the cookies into the green sugar and cover completely. Attach the sugared cookies to the frosted cupcakes, sugar side up, allowing one third of the cookie to hang over the edge.

4. For the eyes, trim the bottom edge of the green cereal pieces. Pipe 2 dots of vanilla frosting at the back of the head and attach the trimmed pieces of cereal, cut side down. Pipe teeth on the outer edges of the heads with the remaining vanilla frosting in the bag, starting at the top edge of the cookie and using the squeeze-release-pull technique (see page 13) to make sharp teeth. Snip a small (1/8-inch) corner from the bag with the black frosting and pipe dots to make the nostrils and eyes.

REEDS

12 mini vanilla cupcakes baked in blue paper liners (see Sources)

1/4 cup granulated sugar

5 candy spearmint leaves (Farley's)

1/2 cup canned vanilla frosting

Neon blue food coloring (McCormick)

1/4 cup blue decorating sugar (see Sources)

1. Sprinkle the granulated sugar on a clean work surface. Roll out the spearmint leaves to a scant 1/4-inch thickness, using additional sugar as necessary to prevent sticking. For the reeds, cut the flattened candies into zigzag grass shapes with clean scissors.

2. Tint the vanilla frosting blue with the food coloring. Spread the blue frosting on top of the mini cupcakes. Place the blue decorating sugar in a small shallow bowl and roll the edge of the cupcakes in the sugar (see page 17). Insert several pieces of the cut spearmint leaves into the frosting as reeds.

3. Arrange the cupcakes on tiered cake stands, with the flamingos above and the hippos and crocs lurking below. Fill in with reeds as desired.

I Thought You Ordered Chocolate Moose

Critters made from candy and cupcakes, what a pair, almonds used as wings, frosting for hair. Circus peanuts for fins, Twinkies for sharks, horses made from creme wafers, with sprinkles for their marks. Cookies for hounds' ears and honeycomb too, a doughnut hole and a fruit chew make a penguin—what a zoo!

Chocolate Moose   86

Hound Dogs   89

March of the Penguins   92

Westies   96

Koi Pond   99

Ants on a Picnic   102

Busy Bees   104

Shark Attack!   108

Crazy Horses   113

candy melting wafers

Tootsie Roll

M&M's Minis

chocolate-covered sunflower seeds

Twinkie

frosting

CHOCOLATE MOOSE

Moose have a reputation for being a little ornery, but under the chocolate coating, this one is just a big Twinkie. I'm sure glad we didn't ask for the baked Alaska.

10 **chocolate cupcakes baked in silver foil liners (Reynolds)**

1¹/₂ **cups dark cocoa candy melting wafers (Wilton)**

10 **creme-filled snack cakes (Twinkies)**

1 **can (16 ounces) plus 1 cup chocolate frosting**

5 **chocolate chews (Tootsie Rolls)**

20 **brown candy-coated chocolate-covered sunflower seeds (Sunny Seed Drops)**

1 **tube (4.25 ounces) white decorating icing (Cake Mate)**

20 **brown mini candy-coated chocolates (M&M's Minis)**

White decorating sugar for serving dishes (see Sources)

1. Place the antler templates (page 88) on a cookie sheet and cover with wax paper.

2. Place the candy melting wafers in a ziplock bag; do not seal. Microwave for 10 seconds to soften. Massage them and return to the microwave. Repeat the process until the candy is smooth, about 60 seconds total (see page 18). Press out the excess air and seal the bag.

3. Snip a small (¹/₈-inch) corner from the bag and pipe the outline of an antler (see page 18). Fill in the antler with melted candy and tap the cookie sheet lightly to smooth the surface. Repeat to make 11 sets of antlers (the extra set is in case of breakage). Refrigerate until set, about 5 minutes.

4. Place a snack cake on its side, flat side facing you, and while holding your knife at an 11 o'clock angle, cut 2 inches off the left bottom corner (keep the larger right side to make the moose). Repeat with the remaining snack cakes.

5. Spread some of the chocolate frosting on top of the cupcakes. Press a trimmed snack cake, cut side down, into the frosting on each cupcake to secure (see photo above). Fill in the gaps at the base of the snack cake with frosting to smooth. Freeze the cupcakes until just firm, 15 to 20 minutes.

6. For the ears, cut the chocolate chews into quarters. Roll or press each piece into a $1/2$-by-1-inch oval, shape one end into a point, and pinch the opposite end. Spoon $1/2$ cup of the remaining chocolate frosting into a ziplock bag, press out the excess air, and seal.

7. Microwave the remaining chocolate frosting in a microwavable 2-cup measuring cup, stopping to stir frequently, until it has the texture of lightly whipped cream,

25 to 35 seconds. Holding a chilled cupcake by the foil liner, dip it into the chocolate frosting up to the liner. Allow the excess frosting to drip off back into the cup (see page 15). Turn right side up, tap the bottom of the cupcake lightly to flatten the frosting, and let stand. If the frosting begins to thicken while you are dipping, reheat it in the microwave for several seconds, stirring well. Allow the cupcakes to dry completely before decorating, about 30 minutes.

8. Carefully peel the chocolate antlers from the wax paper. Insert a set of antlers near the top edge of a cupcake at a slight angle. Snip a small (1/8-inch) corner from the bag with the chocolate frosting. Pipe dots of the chocolate frosting on the tip of the muzzle and attach the sunflower seeds as the nostrils. Pipe a mouth, beard, and tufts of fur between the antlers with the chocolate frosting. Poke a small hole with a toothpick in front of each antler and insert the chocolate ears, pinched end in. Pipe a dot of white icing on either side of the snack cake in front of the ears and attach the mini chocolates as the eyes. Pipe a small white highlight on each eye. Repeat with the remaining cupcakes.

9. Place each cupcake in a dish and fill the dish with white decorating sugar to keep the cupcake balanced.

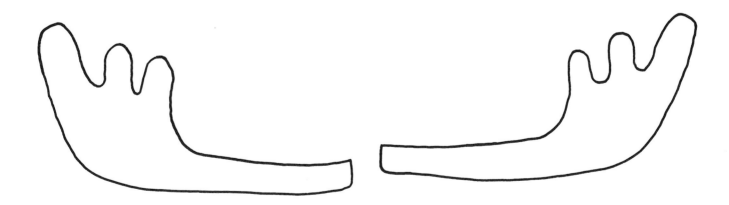

HOUND DOGS

You ain't nothin' but a . . . dachshund, four cupcakes long, dipped in melted frosting, with M&M eyes watching over a bone. And those custom cookie ears, snouts, and tails leave us all shook up.

8 chocolate cupcakes baked in brown paper liners (see Sources)

1/2 recipe dough from Chocolate Sugar Cookies (page 225)

1 cup canned chocolate frosting

1 tube (4.25 ounces) each brown and white decorating icing (Cake Mate)

4 brown candy-coated chocolates (M&M's)

2 black jelly beans

8 chocolate-covered almonds

1/2 cup oat cereal O's (Cheerios; optional)

Dog bone–shaped graham cracker (Scooby-Doo Graham Cracker Stick or cut from cookie dough above; optional)

1. Preheat the oven to 350°F and line a cookie sheet with parchment paper.

2. Using the templates on page 91, cut out the faces, ears, and tails from the rolled-out cookie dough, following the directions on page 20. Bake until the cookies are firm to the touch and fragrant, 8 to 10 minutes. Transfer to a wire rack and cool completely.

3. Spoon the chocolate frosting into a shallow microwavable bowl. Heat the frosting in the microwave, stopping to stir frequently, until it has the texture of lightly whipped cream, 10 to 15 seconds.

4. Holding a cupcake by its paper liner, dip it into the frosting just up to the edge of the liner. Allow the excess frosting to drip off back into the bowl (see page 15). Carefully invert the cupcake and place on a cookie sheet. Repeat with the remaining cupcakes. If the frosting becomes too thick, microwave for several seconds, and stir.

5. Arrange 4 cupcakes in a row on a serving platter. Attach the head cookie and the ears and tail, securing them with a few dots of the brown decorating icing. Pipe several dots of brown icing and attach the brown candies for the eyes and a black jelly bean for the nose. Pipe a few lines of the brown icing for eyebrows. Pipe a white highlight on each eye with the white icing. Arrange the chocolate-covered almonds as the paws along the base of the cupcakes. Repeat with the remaining 4 cupcakes. Use the cereal as dog food and give your dog a bone, if desired.

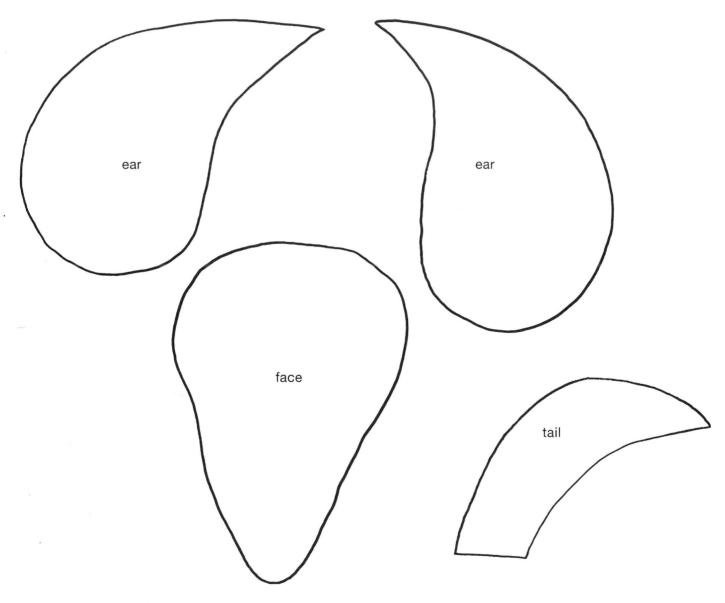

ear

ear

face

tail

MARCH OF THE PENGUINS

Penguins are popping up everywhere from Antarctica to Hollywood. And making a penguin cupcake is no more difficult than placing a mini doughnut and a doughnut hole on top of a cupcake. The last penguin home pulls a bucket filled with the catch of the day.

12 vanilla cupcakes, 11 baked in white paper liners and 1 baked in a silver foil liner (Reynolds)

PENGUINS

4 plain mini doughnuts

1 can (16 ounces) vanilla frosting

7 plain doughnut holes

1 can (16 ounces) dark chocolate frosting

Black food coloring (see Sources)

4 marshmallows

7 thin chocolate cookies (Famous Chocolate Wafers)

7 yellow fruit chews (Starburst, Laffy Taffy)

14 mini chocolate chips

ICEBERGS AND BUCKET

1 cup flaked sweetened coconut

1/2 cup blue and white rock candy, plus more for garnish (see Sources)

Small colored fish candies (see Sources)

1 strand black licorice lace

PENGUINS

1. Cut the mini doughnuts in half crosswise. Spoon 2 tablespoons of the vanilla frosting into a small ziplock bag, press out the excess air, seal, and set aside. Spread vanilla frosting on 7 of the cupcakes and place a mini doughnut half, cut side down, on top. Spread more vanilla frosting on top of the mini doughnut and place a doughnut hole on top. Spread more vanilla frosting up the sides of the doughnut holes to fill the gap as smoothly as possible (see page 14). Place the cupcakes in the freezer for 10 minutes, until slightly frozen.

2. Tint the dark chocolate frosting black with the food coloring. Microwave in a 1- to 2-cup microwavable measuring cup, stirring frequently, until it is the texture of lightly whipped cream, about 35 seconds total. Holding 1 chilled cupcake by its paper bottom, dip it into the black frosting just up to the liner. Hold the cupcake above the surface and allow the excess frosting to drip off (see page 15). Turn right side up and let stand. Repeat with the remaining 6 cupcakes. If the frosting becomes too thick for dipping, reheat for several seconds in the microwave, stirring well.

3. Using clean scissors, cut $1/8$ inch off both flat ends of each marshmallow. Trim $1/4$ inch off one side of 7 of the marshmallow circles to create a straight edge. Press 1 cut marshmallow piece onto the black frosting on each cupcake, straight edge next to the paper liner, to make the penguin's belly.

4. Using a serrated knife, make 2 parallel cuts in each chocolate cookie $1/2$ inch in from opposite sides. The 2 curved outside pieces will form the penguin's wings. Trim $1/4$ inch from one end of each wing. Press the trimmed end of the cookie into the frosting just below the penguin's head, one on each side, securing them with a dot of black frosting.

5. Cut 4 of the yellow fruit chews in half on the diagonal to form the triangular beaks. For each penguin, place the cut side of one of the triangles onto the black frosted doughnut hole, pressing gently to secure. Cut and shape the remaining $3 1/2$ fruit chews into fourteen 3-toed feet. Snip a $1/8$-inch corner from the bag with the vanilla frosting. Pipe white dots for the eyes and add the chocolate chips, pointed end in. Pipe a small white highlight on each eye.

ICEBERGS AND BUCKET

1. Spread the remaining vanilla frosting on top of the remaining 5 cupcakes and press the shredded coconut into the frosting. Arrange the rock candy on top of 4 of the cupcakes in the paper liners to make the ice.

2. Add a few fish candies and the licorice lace to the remaining cupcake in the foil liner. Attach the other end of the licorice to one of the penguins to make his catch of the day.

3. Arrange the penguin cupcakes in a curved line on a serving platter. Place 2 fruit-chew feet in front of each penguin. Place the iceberg cupcakes around the penguins and sprinkle the serving platter with fish candy and rock candy. Tuck a fish candy under the wing of one of the penguins.

i thought you ordered chocolate moose ● 95

WESTIES

With mini cupcake heads and marshmallow snouts, these dogs are all bite and no bark. Snip a corner from a ziplock bag filled with tinted frosting and use it to make the shaggy fur coats in white, tan, and gray. The ears are made from mini marshmallows cut in half and coated on the cut side with sparkling pink sugar.

6 **standard vanilla cupcakes baked in white paper liners**

6 **mini vanilla cupcakes baked in white paper liners**

1 **can (16 ounces) vanilla frosting**

   Brown, yellow, and black food coloring (see Sources)

12 **mini marshmallows**

1 **tablespoon pink decorating sugar (see Sources)**

18 **black candy-coated chocolate-covered sunflower seeds (Sunny Seed Drops)**

6 **strands red licorice laces**

2 **pink fruit chews (Starburst, Tootsie Fruit Rolls)**

1. Spoon $1/3$ cup of the vanilla frosting into a ziplock bag, press out the excess air, and seal. Tint $1/3$ cup of the vanilla frosting light tan with the brown and yellow food coloring and spoon it into a ziplock bag, press out the excess air, and seal. Tint $1/3$ cup of the vanilla frosting light gray with the black food coloring and spoon it into a ziplock bag, press out the excess air, and seal.

2. Cut 6 of the mini marshmallows in half on the diagonal to make the ears and press the cut sides into the pink sugar to coat. Cut the remaining 6 marshmallows on the diagonal to remove one third of the marshmallow. The larger piece will be used to make the muzzles.

3. Start with the heads; work with one color frosting at a time. Snip a small $1/8$-inch corner from the bag of frosting. Pipe a small dot of frosting on the lower half

of a mini cupcake, just below the center. Press a large piece of marshmallow, pointed side up, onto the frosting for the muzzle. Pipe two dots of frosting on opposite sides near the top of the cupcake and attach the ears, sugared side facing forward. Pipe several lines of frosting to cover the non-sugared portion of the ears. Then, starting at one ear, pipe 1/2-inch strokes of frosting around the edge of the cupcake, working your way below the muzzle and up to the other ear, always pulling the frosting away from the center. Next, start at the top of the head and pipe long lines, first to the left, then to the right, working your way down to the marshmallow, then covering the sides of the marshmallow snout. Pipe smaller lines on the front of the marshmallow (leave the marshmallow exposed on the white Westie). Pipe small tufts of hair between the ears. Add 2 of the black sunflower seeds for the eyes and one for the nose. Repeat with the remaining mini cupcakes to make two of each color, six total.

4. Now make the body, using one of the standard cupcakes and the frosting that matches the head. Start piping about 1/2 inch in from the edge using the squeeze-release-pull technique (see page 13) and work your way around the cupcake. Continue piping rows in concentric circles until the cupcake is covered. Continue with the remaining standard size cupcakes to make two bodies in each color, six total.

5. Turn the decorated head in a matching color on its side and place on the body. Add a licorice lace for the leash.

6. Cut each fruit chew into thirds. Form one piece into a teardrop shape for the tongue. Press a knife onto the center of it, lengthwise, to create a crease, and pinch one end. Position the tongue under the bottom side of the snout and push into the frosting to secure. Repeat with the remaining pieces of fruit chew.

KOI POND

CUPCAKE

Koi goldfish made from circus peanuts transform a simple platter of cupcakes into a golden pond. The fish float on overlapping blue and white paper bubbles for a very coy look.

24 vanilla cupcakes baked in blue paper liners (see Sources)

1 can (16 ounces) plus ½ cup vanilla frosting

Blue food coloring

48 orange circus peanuts

48 orange candy-coated chocolates (M&M's)

24 orange cereal O's (Froot Loops, Apple Jacks)

48 brown mini candy-coated chocolates (M&M's Minis)

White and blue paper circles (optional)

White and light blue candy-coated chocolates for serving (My M&M's; optional)

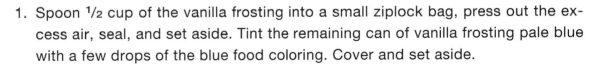

1. Spoon ½ cup of the vanilla frosting into a small ziplock bag, press out the excess air, seal, and set aside. Tint the remaining can of vanilla frosting pale blue with a few drops of the blue food coloring. Cover and set aside.

2. For the fins, place 24 of the circus peanuts on their sides and cut lengthwise into 2 slices, to make 48 slices. Lay each slice cut side down and cut each in half on the diagonal to make 96 pieces. For the bodies, place the remaining 24 circus peanuts flat side down and make a diagonal cut from one end, removing no more than ¼ inch (see photo, page 101).

3. Spread the tops of the cupcakes with the light blue frosting and smooth. Place 1 of the circus peanut bodies on top of each frosted cupcake. Arrange fins, cut side up and pointed ends out, 2 at the uncut end of each circus peanut body and 2 on either side in the middle.

4. Snip a small (1/8-inch) corner from the bag with the vanilla frosting. Pipe a large dot of frosting at the cut end of the circus peanut body. Press 2 orange candies into the dot of frosting for the eyes and 1 cereal O for the mouth. Pipe small dots of vanilla frosting on the orange candies and add the brown candies for the pupils. Repeat on all of the koi bodies with the remaining frosting and candies.

5. If you like, arrange the cupcakes on a surface with circles cut from white and blue papers and sprinkle the platter with white and light blue candies.

ANTS ON A PICNIC

CUPCAKE

The ants come marching one by one, but they leave paired with watermelon slices stacked on their M&M backs. We hear they can lift fruit slices twenty times their own weight on those frosting legs.

12 **vanilla cupcakes baked in green paper liners (see Sources)**

4 **green and 4 red candy fruit slices**

1 **cup flaked sweetened coconut**

Green and yellow food coloring

1/2 **cup canned dark chocolate frosting**

1 **can (16 ounces) vanilla frosting**

36 **brown candy-coated chocolate-covered almonds (M&M's Almond, Brach's Bridge Mix)**

1. For the watermelon rind, use a 1½-inch round cookie cutter or a paring knife to cut out a semicircle from each green fruit slice; reserve the outside edge. For the watermelon flesh, repeat with the red fruit slices and reserve the center areas. Insert the insides from the red fruit slices into the outsides from the green fruit slices to make the watermelons. Cut ¼ inch from the top straight edge through both the green and red pieces.

2. Pulse the coconut in a food processor until finely chopped. Transfer the coconut to a ziplock bag. Add 3 drops of green food coloring and 1 drop of yellow. Seal the bag and shake vigorously until the coconut is tinted grass green (see page 16). Place the coconut in a shallow bowl.

3. Spoon the dark chocolate frosting into a ziplock bag, press out the excess air, and seal.

4. Tint the vanilla frosting spring green with green food coloring and a few drops of yellow. Spread the top of a cupcake with the green frosting and smooth. Roll the edge of the cupcake in the coconut (see page 17). Repeat with the remaining cupcakes and frosting.

5. Snip a small (¹/₈-inch) corner from the bag with the chocolate frosting. Arrange 3 brown candies in a row on top of each cupcake, securing with a dot of chocolate frosting between the candies. Pipe 3 jointed legs on each side of each center candy (see "flying" straight lines, page 13). Pipe 2 chocolate antennae on each head. Pipe chocolate dots to look like seeds on the watermelon candies. Pipe a dot of chocolate frosting on the center candy of 4 of the ants and attach the watermelon slices. Arrange the cupcakes so the ants are marching in a row.

BUSY BEES

Let's get buzzy! We created a honeycomb from hexagonal cookies using custom-made cookie cutters, pressed the cookies into frosting, and filled the centers with honey. Our busy bees are made from black jelly beans, a drizzle of yellow frosting, and sliced almonds.

13 vanilla cupcakes baked in yellow paper liners (see Sources)

¹/₂ recipe dough from Quick Sugar Cookies (page 225)

¹/₂ cup yellow decorating sugar (see Sources)

3 tablespoons light corn syrup

1 can (16 ounces) vanilla frosting

Yellow and black food coloring (see Sources)

17 large black jelly beans (Farley's)

¹/₄ cup sliced almonds (pick through to find the best shapes)

³/₄ cup honey

1. Preheat the oven to 350°F and line a cookie sheet with parchment paper.

2. Using a small paring knife or a homemade cookie cutter made from the larger template (page 107), cut the rolled-out dough into the larger honeycomb shapes (see the photo on page 106). Transfer the cutouts to the cookie sheet, about 1 inch apart. Cut out the centers of the honeycomb shapes with a small paring knife or a homemade cookie cutter made from the smaller template, remove the center dough from each, and reroll the scraps as necessary. Bake the cookies until firm to the touch and lightly golden, about 10 minutes. Transfer to a wire rack and cool completely.

3. Place the yellow sugar in a shallow bowl. Microwave the corn syrup in a microwavable bowl until boiling, 5 to 10 seconds. Brush the top of one of the cooled cookies with the corn syrup and dip into the yellow sugar to coat. (The cookies can be made up to 2 days in advance and kept in an airtight container.)

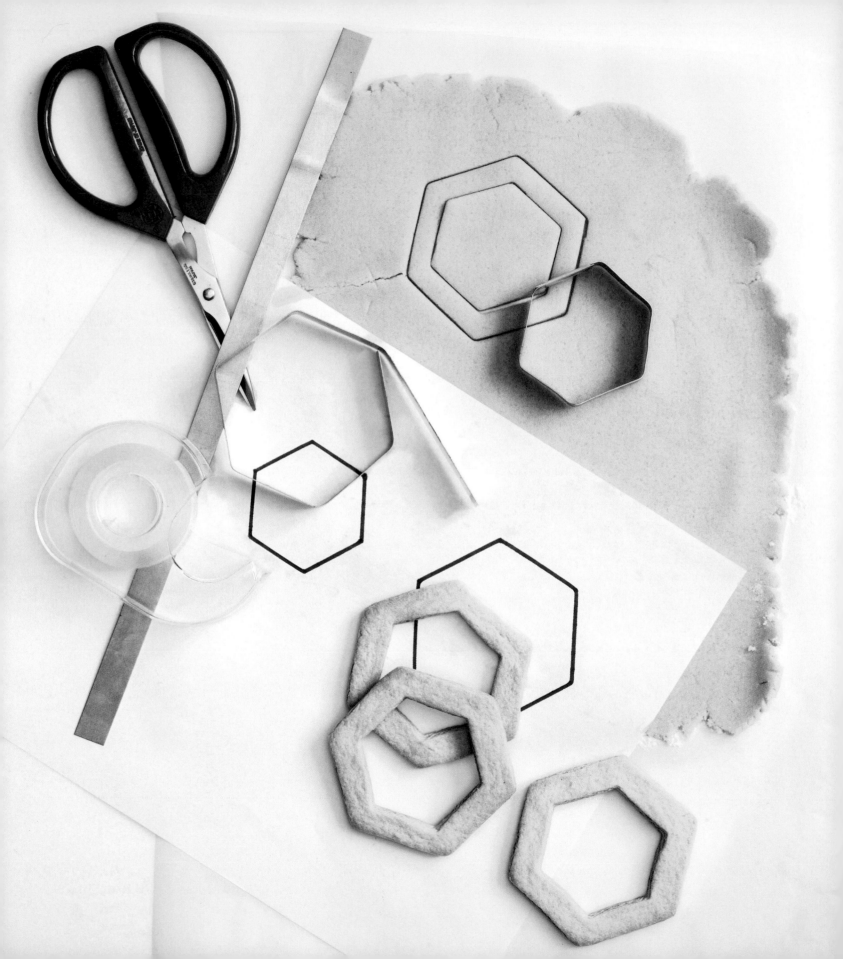

4. Tint ¼ cup of the vanilla frosting yellow and ¼ cup black with the food coloring. Spoon each color into a separate ziplock bag. Spread the tops of the cupcakes with the remaining vanilla frosting and smooth. Place the cookies on top of the cupcakes, sugared side up, pressing them into the frosting to seal any gaps.

5. Arrange 5 cupcakes on a serving platter in a center row, flat sides of the cookies touching. To create the honeycomb, place 4 cupcakes in rows on either side, positioning the cookies to fill in the gaps between the cupcakes in the center row. Level the cookies so they touch at the sides and check for gaps between cookies and frosting.

6. Snip a very small (¹⁄₁₆-inch) corner from the bags with the yellow and black frostings. For the bees, pipe 17 dots of black frosting randomly over the sugared cookies and attach the jelly beans. Pipe a zigzag line of yellow frosting on top of each jelly bean. Add 2 sliced almonds on each side of the jelly beans as wings, pressing them into the frosting to secure. Pipe a black dot of frosting for the head and a small pulled dot for the stinger (see page 13).

7. Just before serving, carefully spoon 2 to 3 teaspoons honey into the center of each honeycomb cookie to come up just to the cookie's edge. Serve immediately.

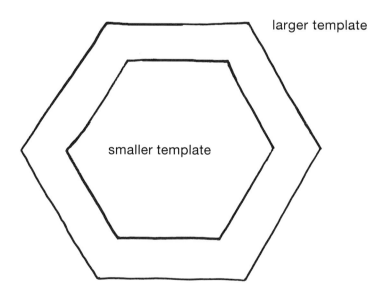

larger template

smaller template

SHARK ATTACK!

Yell "Shark!", arm yourself with a fork, and dive right in. In this eat-or-get-eaten cupcake project, the man-eaters boast a Twinkies center, with razor-sharp frosting teeth and a chocolate wafer back fin. The channel markers and chomped-on life preservers are straight out of a scene from *Jaws: The Cupcake Returns.*

11 vanilla cupcakes baked in blue paper liners (see Sources)

2 cans (16 ounces each) vanilla frosting

Black and blue food coloring (see Sources)

Spoon $1/2$ cup of the vanilla frosting into a ziplock bag, press out the excess air, and seal. Spoon $1/2$ cup of the vanilla frosting into a 1-cup glass measuring cup. Tint $1\frac{1}{2}$ cups of the vanilla frosting light gray with the black food coloring and spoon into a 2-cup glass measuring cup or a small glass bowl. Tint 2 table-spoons of the frosting black with the food coloring and spoon it into a small ziplock bag. Press out the excess air and seal the bag. Tint the remaining frosting light blue with the food coloring.

FOR THE LIFE PRESERVERS
Makes 3 life-preserver cupcakes

3 plain mini doughnuts

Red fruit leather (Fruit by the Foot)

1. Place the mini doughnuts on a wire rack over a cookie sheet lined with wax paper.

2. Microwave the vanilla frosting in the 1-cup measuring cup, stirring frequently, until the frosting is the texture of lightly whipped cream, 10 to 20 seconds. Pour the frosting over the doughnuts to cover completely. Reuse the drippings and reheat if necessary. Refrigerate the doughnuts until set, about 30 minutes.

3. Cut the fruit leather into nine ⅛-by-2½-inch strips. Moisten the back of each strip with a drop of water and wrap 3 strips around each doughnut life preserver as ropes. Use a small fork to remove a bite from the life preserver, if desired.

4. Spread blue frosting on top of 3 of the cupcakes and swirl with the back of a small spoon to create waves. Place 1 life preserver on each cupcake.

FOR THE SHARKS
Makes 3 shark cupcakes

3 creme-filled snack cakes (Twinkies)

2 thin chocolate cookies (Famous Chocolate Wafers)

Red fruit leather (Fruit by the Foot)

6 mini chocolate chips

1. Place a snack cake on its side, flat side facing you, and holding your knife at an angle, cut 1 inch off the bottom corner. Turn the cake back onto its flat side and trim a small wedge off each side of the uncut end to create a slight V-shape for the shark's snout. Repeat with the remaining 2 cakes. Using a serrated knife, cut the chocolate wafers in half.

2. Spread some of the blue frosting on top of 3 of the cupcakes. Press 1 trimmed snack cake, snout end up, into the frosting on each cupcake. Using a small paring knife, cut a 1-inch slit lengthwise in the lower half of each snack cake (along the shark's spine). Insert 1 chocolate wafer half, flat edge down, 1 inch into the slit to make the fin. Freeze the cupcakes until just firm, 10 to 15 minutes.

3. Cut the red fruit leather into three 1-by-2-inch ovals for the shark mouths and set aside.

4. Microwave the gray frosting in the measuring cup, stirring frequently, until it is the texture of lightly whipped cream, 20 to 30 seconds. Holding a chilled cupcake by the paper liner, dip it into the gray frosting to coat the shark and fin completely. Lift the cupcake above the surface and allow the excess frosting to drip off (see page 15). Turn right side up and let stand. If the frosting begins to thicken while you're dipping, reheat it in the microwave for several seconds, stirring well.

5. Press the oval-shaped fruit-leather mouth onto the front of the shark's snout. Snip a 1/8-inch corner from the ziplock bag with the vanilla frosting. Pipe the teeth along the top and bottom edge of the fruit leather, using the squeeze-release-pull technique (see page 13). Press a chocolate chip, flat side up, on each side of the head for the eyes. Snip a 1/16-inch corner from the ziplock bag with the black frosting and pipe 3 gills on each side.

6. Spread blue frosting on each cupcake around the base of the shark and swirl with the back of a small spoon to make waves.

SCHOOL OF FISH
Makes 1 school-of-fish cupcake

1 chocolate-covered marshmallow cookie (Mallomar)

8 red mini gummy fish

1. Spread a small amount of blue frosting on top of the cupcake. Press the marshmallow cookie securely into the frosting, flat side down.

2. Spread more blue frosting on the cupcake and cover the cookie completely. Swirl the frosting with the back of a small spoon to create waves.

3. Press the gummy fish into the frosting, all facing the same direction.

FLOATS
Makes 2 float cupcakes

4 colored spice drops

2 thin pretzel sticks (Rold Gold)

1. Press the flat sides of 2 different-colored spice drops together. Push the pretzel stick through the center of the stacked spice drops, leaving about 1 inch of the pretzel showing at the top.

2. Spread blue frosting on top of 2 of the cupcakes and swirl with the back of a small spoon to make waves. Insert the longer end of one of the pretzel-stick floats into each cupcake at a slight angle.

CHANNEL MARKERS
Makes 2 channel-marker cupcakes

1 tablespoon light corn syrup

2 mini ice cream cones (Joy Kids Cones)

1 tablespoon each red and green decorating sugar (see Sources)

2 red mini lollipops (Dum Dum Pops, Tootsie Pops Miniatures)

1. Microwave the corn syrup in a small bowl until bubbly, about 5 seconds. Brush the outside of the mini cones with the hot corn syrup. Sprinkle 1 cone with green sugar to coat and 1 cone with red sugar. Holding the cone upside down, use a round toothpick to make a small hole in the bottom.

2. Unwrap and insert a lollipop into the hole in each cone. Spread blue frosting on top of the cupcakes and swirl with the back of a small spoon to make waves. Press 1 mini cone, lollipop end up, into the frosting on each cupcake. Using the ziplock bag with the vanilla frosting, pipe a number on the side of each cone.

CRAZY HORSES

Whether you're into Mister Ed, Black Beauty, Seabiscuit, or My Friend Flicka, you'll find a crème wafer in a color to match your circus peanuts. Customize your horses with frosting and sprinkles. You can feed your champions whatever you want, but our ponies like chomping on potato-stick hay.

6 vanilla cupcakes baked in white paper liners

6 chocolate cupcakes baked in brown paper liners (see Sources)

1/2 cup chocolate melting wafers (Wilton)

1/2 cup white chocolate melting wafers (Wilton)

12 chocolate creme wafers (3 1/2 inches long)

12 vanilla creme wafers (3 1/2 inches long)

12 circus peanuts (white, orange, yellow, or pink)

3 tablespoons each white and chocolate sprinkles (see Sources)

1 can (16 ounces) vanilla frosting

1 can (16 ounces) chocolate frosting

6 twist pretzels

Speckled jelly beans (Jelly Belly) and potato sticks for garnish

1. Line a cookie sheet with wax paper. Place the chocolate and white chocolate melting wafers into separate ziplock bags. Do not seal the bags. Microwave for 10 seconds to soften. Massage the chocolates in the bags, return to the microwave, and repeat the process until the chocolate is smooth, about 45 seconds total (see page 18). Press out the excess air and seal the bags.

2. Snip a ¹/₈-inch corner from each of the bags. Pipe a line of chocolate on one of the flat sides of a chocolate creme wafer. Sandwich another chocolate creme wafer on top and place on the cookie sheet. Repeat with the remaining wafers, using the white chocolate for the vanilla creme wafers. Refrigerate until set, about 5 minutes.

3. For the necks, use a serrated knife to cut diagonally across one end of each pair of creme wafers. For the heads, place the circus peanuts on their sides, flat side facing you, hold your knife at an angle, and cut off a ³/₄-inch bottom corner. Pipe melted chocolate (either color) on the cut ends of the peanuts. Attach the peanut heads to the cut ends of the creme wafers. Using either color, pipe spots of melted chocolate on one side of the wafers and add sprinkles (any color) while the chocolate is still liquid. Refrigerate until set, about 5 minutes. Turn the wafers over, pipe spots of melted chocolate on the other side, and add sprinkles. Refrigerate until set, about 5 minutes.

4. Spoon ¹/₂ cup each of the vanilla and chocolate frosting into separate ziplock bags, press out the excess air, and seal. Spread the remaining vanilla frosting on top of the vanilla cupcakes and the chocolate frosting on top of the chocolate cupcakes, mounding the frosting slightly in the center.

5. Insert a small knife into the top of each cupcake, slightly off to the side. Press 1 creme-wafer neck all the way into the slit in each cupcake at an angle. Snip a ¹/₈-inch corner from the bags of vanilla and chocolate frosting. Pipe spots on the cupcakes using either frosting. Add sprinkles where desired. Pipe ears on top of each peanut head using the squeeze-release-pull technique (see page 13). For the mane, pipe short strokes down the top of the neck by squeezing the bag, then releasing and drawing the frosting away from the neck. Pipe a couple of strokes from between the ears onto the forehead. Pipe chocolate dots for the eyes and nostrils.

6. Using a serrated knife, cut off the 2 rounded sides of each twist pretzel and use the curved pieces for the tails. Insert the tail at the edge of the cupcake. Pipe lines of frosting over the pretzel to cover it.

7. Arrange the horse cupcakes on a platter. Scatter the jelly beans around the cupcakes and stack the potato sticks to make the hay.

Let's Party, Cupcake!

There's a pattern at this party: rubber ducks for a shower, Oreos with petals for the sweetest sunflower. A garden with veggies all planted in a row, an apple for the teach made by moms in the know. With golf links for Dad, mums for Mom too, the pattern at this party is, there's a cupcake in it for you.

I'm Seeing a Pattern   118

An Apple a Day   120

Sunflowers   123

Sweet Talk   126

Rubber Ducky   129

Baby Shower   132

Easter Eggs   136

Garden Party   139

Mum's the Word   144

Head of the Class   146

Nineteenth Hole   149

candy-coated
sunflower seeds

blue frosting

I'M SEEING A PATTERN

Whether your inspiration is a fabric, a wallpaper, or a party motif, find a pattern that interests you and study it for candy possibilities. Let your inner design guru lead you to a beautiful cupcake that celebrates your event. Follow the examples here or, better yet, find your own patterns to craft from candy.

FOR THE BLUE FLOWERS AND LEAVES: Frost the cupcakes with chocolate frosting. Tint vanilla frosting pale blue, place it in a ziplock bag, and follow the fabric for inspiration, piping the curving stems and leaves. Finally, add pale blue candy-coated chocolate-covered sunflower seeds and frosting to make the flowers.

FOR THE CHOCOLATE DOTS: Frost the cupcakes with a light tan frosting to match the fabric and place brown M&M's Minis in diagonal rows to match the pattern.

AN APPLE A DAY

Whether you want to put Snow White to sleep, butter up the teacher, keep the doctor away, or tempt Adam's fate, our apples will do the trick. They're made from doughnuts coated in red frosting, rolled in red sugar, and adorned with Tootsie Roll stems and fruit chew leaves.

8 **vanilla cupcakes baked in red paper liners (see Sources)**

1 **can (16 ounces) vanilla frosting**

Red paste food coloring (Wilton)

8 **mini plain or chocolate-frosted doughnuts**

4 **chocolate chews (Tootsie Rolls)**

6 **green fruit chews (Jolly Rancher, Tootsie Fruit Rolls)**

1 **cup red decorating sugar (see Sources)**

3 **black candy-coated chocolate-covered sunflower seeds (Sunny Seed Drops)**

1. Spoon 1 tablespoon of the vanilla frosting into a small ziplock bag, press out the excess air, and seal. Tint the remaining vanilla frosting red with the food coloring. Cut 1/2 inch from the bottom of each mini doughnut with a serrated knife and discard the bottom piece. Spread some red frosting on the cupcakes and place the mini doughnut piece, cut side down, on top (see photo, page 122). Place the cupcakes in the freezer for 10 minutes, or until slightly frozen.

2. For the stems, cut the chocolate chews in half lengthwise on the diagonal and shape each half into a stem. For the leaves, roll out the green fruit chews to a 1/8-inch thickness, and then cut into twelve 3/4-by-1 1/2-inch leaf shapes. Make a crease down the center of each leaf with the back of a paring knife and pinch one end.

3. Place the red decorating sugar in a medium shallow bowl. Working on 1 cupcake at a time, spread some of the red frosting on the top and sides of the doughnut and cupcake to fill in the gaps and lightly coat, making the doughnut top look like the top of an apple. Roll the frosted cupcake in the red sugar to coat (see page 17). Repeat with the remaining cupcakes.

4. To create a bite mark, carefully remove a 1½-inch-diameter divot in the side of 1 sugar-coated doughnut, using the tines of a fork or a paring knife. Snip a small (⅛-inch) corner from the bag with the vanilla frosting and pipe a thin layer of frosting to cover the exposed area inside the divot. Spread lightly with the back of a small spoon to smooth. Arrange the sunflower seeds in the vanilla frosting as the apple seeds, pointed ends toward the center. Insert the chocolate chew stems with the green fruit chew leaves at the top of the apple cupcakes. Arrange the cupcakes in a basket.

SUNFLOWERS

CUPCAKE

The petals on these bright, sassy cupcakes may look complicated but are actually quick and easy: just grab a ziplock bag filled with 2 colors of frosting and squeeze, pull, and release. Practice makes perfect.

24 **vanilla cupcakes baked in green paper lIners (see Sources)**

2 **cans (16 ounces each) vanilla frosting**

Green, yellow, orange, and black food coloring (see Sources)

14–16 **chocolate cream-filled sandwich cookies Oreos)**

25–30 **mini chocolate cream-filled sandwich cookies (Mini Oreos)**

$1/2$ **cup granulated sugar**

15–20 **candy spearmint leaves (Farley's) or 2 rolls green fruit leather (Fruit by the Foot)**

2 **tablespoons dark chocolate frosting**

6–10 **red candy-coated chocolates (M&M's)**

Basket lined with green tissue paper (optional)

1. Tint $1\frac{1}{2}$ cups of the vanilla frosting green with the food coloring. Spread an even layer of the green frosting on top of the cupcakes and smooth. Arrange the chocolate sandwich cookies, regular and mini, randomly over the cupcakes, pressing them into the frosting to secure.

2. Tint the remaining vanilla frosting bright yellow with the food coloring. Remove $1/2$ cup of the yellow frosting and tint it orange with the food coloring. Spoon $1/4$ cup of the orange frosting into one side of a ziplock bag and spoon half of the yellow frosting into the other side of the bag. Press out the excess air and seal the bag. Repeat the process with another ziplock bag and the remaining orange and yellow frosting. Reinforce the corner of each bag with 6 overlapping layers of Scotch tape (see photo page 124). Pinch the taped corners flat and cut a small V-shape in the corner to make a leaf tip (see photo page 124). Pipe

yellow-orange frosting around the edge of each cookie to make petals using the squeeze-release-pull technique (see page 13). Pipe another circle of petals just inside the first and slightly overlapping.

3. Sprinkle the work surface with the sugar. Roll out the spearmint leaves, if using, one at a time, to 1/8 inch thick. Using clean scissors, cut the candies or fruit leather into 1 1/2-inch-long leaf shapes. Press the leaves into the cupcakes just under the petals.

4. Tint the chocolate frosting black with the food coloring and spoon it into a small zi-plock bag. Press out the excess air and seal the bag. Snip a 1/16-inch corner from the bag. Pipe a dot of black frosting on some of the cookies and attach the red chocolate candies to make the ladybugs. Pipe a line of black frosting down the center of each ladybug and add a dot for the head and a few dots on the back.

5. Arrange the cupcakes close together in a basket lined with green tissue paper, if you like, in small cups or on a platter.

SWEET TALK

Express yourself on a heart cut from pound cake dipped in melted pastel-colored frosting. Our message to you: everything sounds sweeter when it's written on a cupcake.

18 vanilla cupcakes baked in white paper liners

3 frozen pound cakes (10.75 ounces each; Sara Lee), thawed

3 cans (16 ounces each) vanilla frosting

Red, green, yellow, orange, and purple food coloring (see Sources)

Conversation heart candies for decorating the platter (Necco Sweethearts)

1. Cut the pound cakes in half horizontally and lay the halves flat. Using a 3-inch heart-shaped cookie cutter, cut out 3 hearts from each half. (Tip: reserve the scraps for a layered dessert.)

2. Spread the top of the cupcakes with some of the vanilla frosting. Place a pound cake heart on top of each cupcake, pressing down to secure. Place the cupcakes in the freezer for 15 minutes, or until slightly frozen.

3. Tint ½ cup of the vanilla frosting red with the food coloring. Spoon the red frosting into a ziplock bag, press out the excess air, seal, and set aside. Divide the remaining frosting among five small microwavable bowls. Tint each bowl a different pastel color of pink, green, yellow, orange, and lavender. Cover with plastic wrap and set aside.

4. Working with one color of frosting at a time, microwave the frosting, stopping to stir frequently, until it has the texture of lightly whipped cream, about 10 sec-

onds. Remove 1 cupcake at a time from the freezer. Holding the cupcake by its paper bottom, dip it into the frosting just to cover the pound cake heart. Allow the excess frosting to drip off back into the bowl (see page 15). Turn right side up and let stand. Repeat with each color and the remaining cupcakes. If the frosting becomes too thick, reheat for several seconds, stirring well. Remove any excess frosting from the base of the hearts if necessary.

5. Snip a very small ($1/16$-inch) corner from the bag with the red frosting. Pipe sayings on top of the hearts. Place on a serving platter. Sprinkle the conversation heart candies around the platter at the base of the cupcakes.

RUBBER DUCKY

Time to get your ducks in a row. These are perfect for a baby shower, a birthday party, or even a crazy Easter bash. Making that ducky shape is as simple as attaching a doughnut hole and a marshmallow to a cupcake. Dip in melted yellow frosting and add a fruit chew beak and M&M eyes, and this little yellow flotilla is ready to quack.

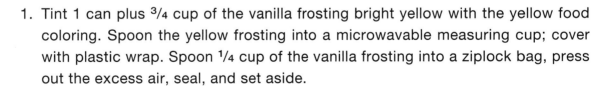

24 vanilla cupcakes baked in yellow paper liners (see Sources)

2 cans (16 ounces each) plus 1 cup vanilla frosting

Yellow food coloring

12 marshmallows

20 plain doughnut holes

14 orange fruit chews (Tootsie Fruit Rolls, Starburst)

48 brown mini candy-coated chocolates (M&M's Minis)

1. Tint 1 can plus $3/4$ cup of the vanilla frosting bright yellow with the yellow food coloring. Spoon the yellow frosting into a microwavable measuring cup; cover with plastic wrap. Spoon $1/4$ cup of the vanilla frosting into a ziplock bag, press out the excess air, seal, and set aside.

2. Cut the marshmallows in half on the diagonal with scissors. Spread some of the vanilla frosting from the remaining can on top of a cupcake. For the head, place a doughnut hole on one side. For the tail, arrange the cut marshmallow, pointed end up, on the edge on the opposite side (see the photo on page 14). Repeat to make 20 heads-up ducks. To make the bottoms-up ducks, place a cut marshmallow in the center of each of the remaining 4 cupcakes, pointed end up. Spread vanilla frosting up the sides of the doughnut holes and marshmallows on the cupcakes to fill in the gaps and smooth. Place the cupcakes in the freezer for 15 minutes, or until slightly frozen.

3. Microwave the yellow frosting, stopping to stir frequently, until it has the texture of lightly whipped cream, about 45 seconds. Remove 1 cupcake at a time from the freezer. Holding the cupcake by its paper bottom, dip it into the yellow frosting just up to the liner. Allow the excess frosting to drip off back into the cup (see page 15). Turn right side up and let stand. Repeat with the remaining cupcakes. If the frosting becomes too thick, reheat for several seconds, stirring well.

4. For the beaks, cut 10 of the orange fruit chews in half. Shape each piece into a ³/₄-by-1¹/₂-inch oval. Fold the fruit chew almost in half, then pinch at the fold and shape to look like an open beak. Place the folded edge of the fruit chew on the front of the doughnut hole head, pressing gently to secure. For the feet, cut the remaining 4 fruit chews in half on the diagonal. Flatten each piece into a 1-by-1¹/₂-by-1¹/₂-inch triangle. Shape the short end to make the webbed feet. Score the top with a small knife. Insert the pointed end of the feet at the base of the tail on the bottoms-up cupcakes. Snip a small (¹/₈-inch) corner from the bag with the vanilla frosting. Pipe a white dot on either side of the head for the eyes and add the mini brown candies.

VARIATION: Beaks and feet can be made from circus peanuts. Place a circus peanut flat side down and cut in half cross-wise. For the beak, place one half on its side. Starting at the round end, make a cut halfway through the candy. Open slightly at the cut end. For the feet, place the other half on its side and cut all the way through. Flatten each piece slightly and cut small notches from the flat end.

BABY SHOWER

Cupcakes are the perfect bring-along for a baby shower. They're easy to pack in a box and just as easy to pass around. Each of these cutie-pies is made from two cupcakes, a mini sitting atop a standard.

15 standard vanilla cupcakes baked in pastel paper liners (see Sources)

15 mini vanilla cupcakes baked in white paper liners

8 pastel mini marshmallows

$1/2$ cup light blue (or pink or yellow) candy melting wafers (Wilton)

2 cans (16 ounces each) vanilla frosting

Red food coloring

$1/2$ cup dark chocolate frosting

1 teaspoon instant coffee (brown food coloring also works but is flavorless)

1 tablespoon warm water

6 red fruit chews (Starburst, Jolly Rancher, Airheads)

1 cup white mini marshmallows

5 bear-shaped graham crackers, honey flavor (Teddy Grahams)

1 6-inch piece red fruit leather (Fruit by the Foot)

1 strand red licorice lace

5 red cereal O's (Froot Loops)

Flower decors

SAFETY PINS
Makes 16 safety pins (1 extra in case of breakage)

1. Using clean scissors, cut the pastel mini marshmallows in half crosswise. With the sticky side down, trim one side of each marshmallow half with scissors to

create a semicircle for the head of the safety pin. Place the template for the safety pin (page 135) on a cookie sheet and cover with wax paper.

2. Place the blue candy melting wafers in a ziplock bag. Do not seal the bag. Microwave for 10 seconds to soften. Massage the wafers in the bag, return to the microwave, and repeat the process until the candy is smooth, about 30 seconds total (see page 18). Press out the excess air and seal the bag. Snip a $^1/_{16}$-inch corner from the bag. Pipe an outline of the safety pin on the wax paper. While the melted candy is still wet, add a trimmed marshmallow piece, curved side in, to the head of the safety pin as the clasp. Repeat the process until you have 16 safety pins. Refrigerate until set, about 5 minutes.

BABIES
Makes 15 babies

1. Spoon $^3/_4$ cup of the vanilla frosting into a ziplock bag. Tint 3 tablespoons of the vanilla frosting red with the food coloring and spoon it into a ziplock bag. Spoon the chocolate frosting into a ziplock bag. Press out the excess air in each of the bags, seal, and set aside. Dissolve the instant coffee in the warm water. Divide the remaining vanilla frosting into 3 separate bowls. Tint one part pale pink with a very small amount of red food coloring, one part pale beige with a few drops of the coffee, and one part tan with a few drops of the coffee and a touch of red food coloring. Cover the frostings with plastic wrap to prevent drying.

2. Snip a $^1/_8$-inch corner from the bag with the vanilla frosting. Cut 1 of the red fruit chews into 5 pieces. For the nipple on the baby bottle, roll each piece into a chocolate chip shape. Pipe a dot of white frosting on one of the flat ends of a white mini marshmallow and attach the nipple. Repeat with the remaining 4 fruit-chew pieces to make 5 baby bottles. Roll out the remaining 5 fruit chews on wax paper to $^1/_8$ inch thick and cut out bibs using the bib template as a guide. Using clean scissors, cut the remaining white mini marshmallows crosswise into thirds.

3. Spread the tops of 5 each of the standard cupcakes and 5 each of the mini cupcakes with the pink, beige, and tan frostings, mounding it slightly. Arrange 7 or 8 pieces of the cut mini marshmallows along the top edge of each of the mini cupcakes to make the bonnet.

4. Pipe a thin, wavy line of vanilla frosting around the edge of each of the standard cupcakes. Carefully peel the candy safety pins from the wax paper and press one pin into the wavy line of frosting at the edge of each standard cupcake.

5. Snip a $^1/_{16}$-inch corner from the bag with the chocolate frosting. Pipe eyelids and eyelashes on the mini cupcakes and a belly button, just above the safety pin, on each of the standard cupcakes. Pipe eyes on the teddy bear graham crackers.

6. Cut five $^3/_4$-inch-long ovals from the red fruit leather and add as the mouth on 5 of the mini cupcakes. Snip a $^1/_{16}$-inch corner from the bag with the red frosting and pipe a line around the edge of each oval. Pipe a red nose on the teddy bears. Cut the red licorice lace into five $1^1/_2$-inch lengths. For each pacifier, press the licorice ends together and insert the ends into the hole in one of the red cereal O's. Press the pacifiers into the frosting on 5 of the mini cupcakes.

7. Matching like colors, place the mini cupcakes on their sides on top of the standard cupcakes, with the frosting facing the safety pin. For the bibbed babies, arrange the head slightly to one side, with the safety pin to the other side. Position the top of the bib at the baby's head. Pipe a few dots of vanilla frosting on the bib and add the flower decors. Add the teddy bears to the open-mouthed babies, securing them with a dot of frosting. Add the bottles to the 5 babies without mouths, pressing the nipple into the frosting.

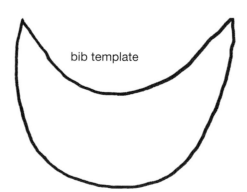

bib template

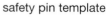

safety pin template

EASTER EGGS

These eggs just may upstage the bunny. The egg-shaped graham crackers are coated with frosting and decorated with sparkling sugars and a rainbow assortment of candies. For half of the cupcakes, the sugar coating goes on first, and for the other half, the candies are applied before the sugar, creating a subtle difference in the brightly colored tones. Just think: when you make these Easter eggs, you can eat cupcakes all week long instead of egg salad sandwiches. How great is that?

12 chocolate cupcakes baked in white paper liners

1 can (16 ounces) plus 1 cup vanilla frosting

Green, yellow, orange, purple, and red food coloring (see Sources)

12 honey graham crackers

1/2 cup each blue, violet, pink, and yellow decorating sugars (see Sources)

2 tablespoons each mini and regular flower decors, mini and regular dot decors, and stick decors (see Sources)

1. Tint 1 1/2 cups of the vanilla frosting light green. Spoon 1 cup of green frosting into a ziplock bag. Reserve the remaining 1/2 cup. Tint 2 tablespoons each of the vanilla frosting yellow, orange, light purple, and pink, and spoon into separate small ziplock bags. Spoon 2 tablespoons of the vanilla frosting into a small ziplock bag. Press out the excess air in each of the bags, seal, and set aside.

2. Using a serrated knife, trim each graham cracker to fit the template shape. Put a small dollop of the green frosting on top of the cupcakes and place 1 graham-cracker egg on each cupcake, pressing down to secure. The crackers will extend over the edge of the cupcakes.

3. Place each color of decorating sugar on a small shallow plate, such as a saucer. Spoon the remaining vanilla frosting into a ziplock bag, press out the excess air, and seal. Snip a $\frac{1}{2}$-inch corner from the bag. Working on one cracker at a time, pipe frosting on top of the cracker and spread it in a smooth, even layer to cover the top. For 6 of the cupcakes, arrange the decors in a pattern on top of the frosting, using tweezers, then carefully roll the top of the cracker in the desired color of sugar to cover completely. For the remaining 6 cupcakes, roll the frosted crackers in the desired color of sugar first, then arrange the decors in a pattern on top of the sugar-coated crackers.

4. Snip a $\frac{1}{16}$-inch corner from the small bags with the yellow, orange, purple, pink, and vanilla frosting. Pipe dots, lines, and dashes of frosting on top of the sugar-coated crackers using the techniques on page 13. Snip a $\frac{1}{8}$-inch corner from the bag with the green frosting and pipe pulled dots of frosting around the base of each egg, covering the top of the cupcake.

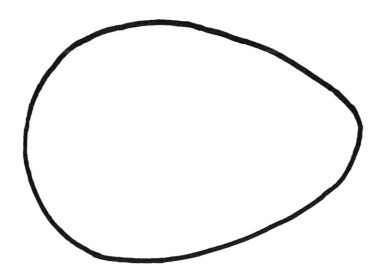

GARDEN PARTY

A garden plan should always include veggies the kids will eat, like candy-coated chocolate peas, taffy radishes, fruit-chew carrots, and frosted-flake lettuce. Our cupcake garden includes rows of freshly turned chocolate earth, chewy licorice vines, and a summer harvest of sweet vegetables sure to please a crowd.

24 vanilla cupcakes baked in white paper liners

2 whole graham crackers

2 sticks mint chewing gum

1/4 cup white chocolate melting wafers (Wilton)

6 thin pretzel sticks (Bachman)

1 cup canned vanilla frosting

Green, red, orange, and blue food coloring (see Sources)

1 can (16 ounces) chocolate frosting

2 cups chocolate cookie crumbs (Oreos, Famous Chocolate Wafers)

1 cup cornflakes

9 green fruit chews (Jolly Rancher)

1 vanilla fruit chew (Tootsie Roll Midgee, Airhead)

4 red fruit chews (Jolly Rancher)

8 orange fruit chews (Starburst)

1 teaspoon ground cinnamon

20 green candy-coated chocolates (M&M's)

Green and yellow licorice laces (see Sources)

2 teaspoons multicolored candy-coated chocolate-covered sunflower seeds (Sunny Seed Drops)

1. Using a serrated knife, cut the graham crackers in half crosswise. Cut each stick of gum into a $^3/_4$-inch-long triangle and pinch on one side to make the shovel blades. Line a cookie sheet with wax paper. Place the white chocolate melting wafers in a ziplock bag. Do not seal the bag. Microwave for 10 seconds to soften. Massage the chocolates in the bag, return to the microwave, and repeat the process until the chocolate is smooth, about 30 seconds total (see page 18). Press out the excess air and seal the bag.

2. Snip a $^1/_8$-inch corner from the bag and pipe an outline around each graham cracker. Fill in with more chocolate and spread into a smooth, thin layer to cover the cracker. Place on the cookie sheet and refrigerate until set, about 5 minutes.

3. Turn each cracker over and pipe a line of melted chocolate down the center of the uncoated side. Place a pretzel stick on top of the line of chocolate, leaving about a 2-inch overhang. Refrigerate until set. Cut the remaining 2 pretzel sticks into two 2-inch and two $^3/_4$-inch lengths. Pipe a small dot of melted chocolate on one end of the 2-inch pretzel stick and attach the smaller pretzel piece crosswise to make the shovel handle. Attach the gum shovel blade to the other end of the pretzel with a dot of melted chocolate. Place on the cookie sheet and refrigerate until set, about 5 minutes.

4. Tint $^1/_2$ cup of the vanilla frosting green with the food coloring. Tint 1 tablespoon of the vanilla frosting red. Tint 2 tablespoons of the vanilla frosting orange. Tint $^1/_4$ cup of the vanilla frosting blue. Spoon each color, including the remaining 1 tablespoon vanilla frosting, into separate ziplock bags, press out the excess air, and seal. Spoon $^1/_4$ cup of the chocolate frosting into a ziplock bag, press out the excess air, and seal. Snip a $^1/_{16}$-inch corner from each of the bags. Pipe the vegetable names in chocolate frosting and the vegetable shapes in the colored frostings on top of the chocolate-coated side of the graham crackers. Pipe a blue line of frosting around the border of each sign.

5. Place the chocolate cookie crumbs in a medium bowl. Spread the remaining chocolate frosting over the tops of the cupcakes. Starting at the edge, roll the tops of the cupcakes in the crumbs to cover completely. Arrange the cupcakes in 4 rows of 6 on a serving platter.

6. Work on one vegetable at a time.

LETTUCE
Makes 4 lettuce cupcakes

Line a cookie sheet with wax paper. Place the cornflakes in a small bowl. Spoon the remaining green frosting into a small microwavable bowl. Microwave the frosting, stirring frequently, until it is smooth and has the texture of lightly whipped cream, 5 to 10 seconds (see page 15). Pour the frosting over the cornflakes, toss well to coat, and spread the cornflakes onto the cookie sheet. Refrigerate until set, about 10 minutes. Cut 2 of the green fruit chews in half and shape into balls. Place 1 green ball on top of each of 4 cupcakes and arrange 8 to 12 green-frosted cornflakes around the balls to make the leaves. Secure with a dot of green frosting, if necessary.

RADISHES
Makes 4 radish cupcakes

For each radish, cut the vanilla fruit chew into quarters. Roll 1 red fruit chew together with 1 vanilla piece, keeping the colors separate, and shape into a ball. Pinch the white end to form the radish root. Place 1 radish on top of each of 4 cupcakes, and add several green-frosted cornflakes for the leaves.

CARROTS
Makes 5 carrot cupcakes

Cut 2 of the orange fruit chews in half and shape each piece into a small carrot. Shape the remaining 6 fruit chews into 6 large carrots. Score the side of each carrot with a knife. Rub the sides of the carrots with the cinnamon to make them look freshly pulled from the garden. Use a round toothpick to make a small hole in the large end of each carrot. Cut 2 of the green fruit chews into thin strips and roll each strip between your fingers to look like carrot tops. Press 4 or 5 strips into the hole in the top of each carrot. Arrange the carrots, overlapping slightly, on top of 5 cupcakes.

PEAS
Makes 5 pea-pod cupcakes

Roll out each of the remaining 5 green fruit chews into a 3-by-1-inch oval $\frac{1}{8}$ inch thick. Press 4 green candy-coated chocolates onto one side of each oval. Fold the other side over to cover the candies slightly. Pinch the ends and place 1 pea pod on top of each of 5 cupcakes. Cut the green and yellow licorice laces into various lengths and arrange them around the pea pods to make the vines.

SHOVELS AND SIGNS
Makes 4 seed-pack cupcakes and 2 shovel cupcakes

Insert the pretzel end of each seed-pack sign into the top of each of 4 cupcakes and place at the head of the rows. Insert the shovel blades into the frosting on top of 2 cupcakes, scatter a few sunflower seeds around the shovels, and place in the rows with the radishes and lettuce.

MUM'S THE WORD

Moms love mums. We cut mini marshmallows on the diagonal and dipped the sticky side in colored sugar to make dozens of pink, yellow, purple, blue, and orange petals. Your mums will leave Mom speechless.

8 vanilla cupcakes baked in orange paper liners (see Sources)

¼ cup each blue, white, light yellow, bright pink, bright yellow, orange, and purple decorating sugars (see Sources; or see page 16 to tint your own)

1 bag (10.5 ounces) flavored mini marshmallows (assorted pastel colors)

1 bag (10.5 ounces) mini marshmallows

1 cup canned vanilla frosting

40 pastel-colored licorice pastels (Jelly Belly)

Green licorice twists (Twizzlers Rainbow Twists)

1. Place each colored sugar in a separate shallow bowl. Sort out 22 like-colored marshmallows for each cupcake. Make the petals for each cupcake by cutting the 22 mini marshmallows in half on the diagonal, allowing all of the marshmallow pieces to fall into one of the colored sugars. Shake the bowl and press the cut sides of the marshmallows into the sugar to coat. Repeat with the remaining marshmallows and colored sugars.

2. Spread a thin layer of frosting on top of 1 cupcake. Starting along the outside edge of the cupcake, arrange like-colored marshmallow petals, sugared sides up, close together. Continue with another 2 rows of the same color marshmallows to almost completely cover the cupcake. Repeat with the remaining frosting, cupcakes, and marshmallows.

3. For the stamens, insert 5 like-colored licorice pastels in the center of each cupcake. Arrange the flower cupcakes on a serving platter. Trim the green licorice twists to look like stems and place on the platter.

HEAD OF THE CLASS

Here's a bird's-eye view of the graduating class. Each cap made from Reese's Peanut Butter Cups and After Eight mints sits atop a unique head of hair—or lack of it—crafted from chewing gum, cereal, frosting, or sugar. Make liners, tassels, and buttons to match your school colors.

10 vanilla cupcakes baked in liners to match school colors (Reynolds)

1 can (16 ounces) vanilla frosting

Yellow, red, and blue food coloring

1 cup canned chocolate frosting

$^1/_4$ teaspoon unsweetened cocoa powder

$^1/_4$ cup each orange, red, and yellow cereal O's (Froot Loops)

12 sticks yellow gum (Juicy Fruit)

3 tablespoons chocolate sprinkles

2 teaspoons white decorating sugar (see Sources)

12 mini chocolate and peanut butter cups (Reese's), unwrapped

12 chocolate-covered thin mint candies or graham crackers (After Eight or Afrika cookies)

10 blue mini candy-coated chocolates (M&M's Minis)

1. Tint $^1/_4$ cup of the vanilla frosting orange with the yellow and red food coloring. Tint 3 tablespoons of the vanilla frosting blue. Spoon each color frosting into a separate ziplock bag. Spoon the chocolate frosting into a ziplock bag, press out the excess air, and seal the bags. Tint the remaining vanilla frosting light tan with red food coloring and the cocoa powder. Cover with plastic wrap and set aside.

2. Frost the cupcakes with a mound of the light tan frosting and smooth. For the ears, press 2 orange cereal O's on opposite sides of each frosted cupcake, just above the paper liner. Add hair as directed on the next page.

FOR SHORT BLOND HAIR: Cut 6 gum sticks in half crosswise. Using pinking shears, cut one short end to create a zigzag end. Using straight scissors, cut long strips, leaving a 1/2-inch section uncut at the straight end. Press the gum pieces into the frosting to create 2 layers of hair.

FOR LONG BLOND HAIR: Using scissors and 4 sticks of the yellow gum, cut lengthwise strips 1/8 inch wide from one short end of each gum stick, leaving 1/2 inch at the other short end uncut. Cut the remaining 2 sticks in half crosswise and cut more thin strips, leaving 1/2 inch at the other short end uncut. Press the long pieces into the frosting at the sides and back of the cupcake and add the short pieces to the front to make bangs.

FOR CURLY HAIR: Starting at the bottom edge of a frosted cupcake, press the red cereal O's into the frosting in overlapping circles, leaving the top empty for the graduation cap. Repeat with the yellow cereal O's and another cupcake.

FOR FROSTING HAIR: Snip a small (1/8-inch) corner from the bags with each of the tinted frostings. To make the curls, pipe the orange frosting all over one cupcake. Repeat with the chocolate frosting and another cupcake. To make shaggy hair, start at the edge of the cupcake and, using the squeeze-release-pull technique (see page 13), pipe rows of hair with the chocolate frosting. To make parted hair, mark a line down the center of a cupcake with a toothpick and pipe rows of chocolate frosting from the center line on either side, leaving a small gap to show the tan frosting.

FOR A CREW CUT: Place the chocolate sprinkles in a small shallow bowl. Roll the frosted cupcake in the sprinkles to cover (see page 17).

FOR A BALD HEAD: Sprinkle the cupcake with the white decorating sugar to cover.

3. Press a chocolate peanut butter cup, large end down, on top of each cupcake, adding a dot of frosting to secure if necessary. Pipe a dot of chocolate frosting on top of each peanut butter cup and add the chocolate-covered mint or cookie as the mortarboard. For the tassel, starting from the center of the mortarboard, pipe several lines of blue frosting, allowing the frosting to overhang the edge of the chocolate. Press a blue candy on top. Arrange the cupcakes on a platter in 2 rows.

NINETEENTH HOLE

By the time you get done with the back nine, it's time to sit back and enjoy a cupcake at the nineteenth hole. Our links include a well-maintained fairway of close-cropped frosting grass, a green that is groomed to perfection with a coating of sugar, and a challenging sand trap filled with vanilla cookie crumbs.

24 vanilla cupcakes, 6 baked in white paper liners and 18 baked in green paper liners (see Sources)

1/2 cup ground vanilla wafers

**2 cans (16 ounces each) vanilla frosting
Green food coloring**

1/2 cup green decorating sugar (see Sources)

1 yellow flat candy (Smarties)

1 yellow licorice pastel (Jelly Belly)

1 tablespoon white nonpareils (see Sources)

4 white gum balls

1 teaspoon light corn syrup

1 2-inch piece strawberry fruit leather (Fruit by the Foot)

1 thin pretzel stick (Bachman)

1 large chocolate chip (Hershey's Mini Kisses)

1. Place the cookie crumbs in a shallow bowl. Spread the tops of the 6 cupcakes in white paper liners with vanilla frosting and smooth. Roll the tops in the crumbs to cover (see page 17). Spoon 2 tablespoons vanilla frosting into a small ziplock bag, press out the excess air, and seal. Tint the remaining frosting green with the food coloring.

2. Place the green decorating sugar in a small shallow bowl. Spread the tops of 7 of the remaining cupcakes with green frosting and smooth. Roll the tops in the

sugar to cover. Spread a thin layer of green frosting over the remaining 11 cupcakes. Spoon the remaining green frosting into two ziplock bags, press out the excess air, and seal.

3. Arrange the cupcakes on a serving platter, grouping the crumb-topped cupcakes and the sugar-topped cupcakes together (see the photo on the opposite page). Snip a small ($\frac{1}{8}$-inch) corner from the bags with the green frosting. Pipe grass over the green-frosted cupcakes and around the perimeter of the sugar-topped cupcakes using the squeeze-release-pull technique (see page 13).

4. For the tee, snip a small ($\frac{1}{8}$-inch) corner from the bag with the vanilla frosting and pipe a dot on one end of the yellow flat candy. Attach the licorice pastel and insert into 1 of the cupcakes at the tee position. Place the white nonpareils in a small shallow bowl. Roll the gum balls in the corn syrup to coat and then roll them in the nonpareils to coat. Place 1 ball on top of the tee and the others on other cupcakes.

5. For the flag, fold the fruit leather in half around one end of the pretzel stick. Using clean scissors, cut into a triangular flag shape. Pipe the number "19" on the flag with the vanilla frosting. Insert the pretzel stick in the center of the sugar-topped cupcake grouping. For the hole, add the large chocolate chip at the base of the pretzel, pointed end down.

The House That Boo Built

A big old haunted house that's chocolate to the core; beware the candy insects, and howling wolves at the door. Chilly ghosts float on dark chocolate dirt, green aliens in spaceships cooked up for dessert. These treats remind us it's that time of year when even the cupcakes give us reason to fear.

The Haunted House   154

Chilly Ghosts   157

Alien Invasion   160

Creepy Crawlers   163

What a Hoot!   167

Jack-O'-Lanterns   170

Mr. Bones Jangle   174

Howling Werewolves   177

Black Cats   180

Larry the Turkey   183

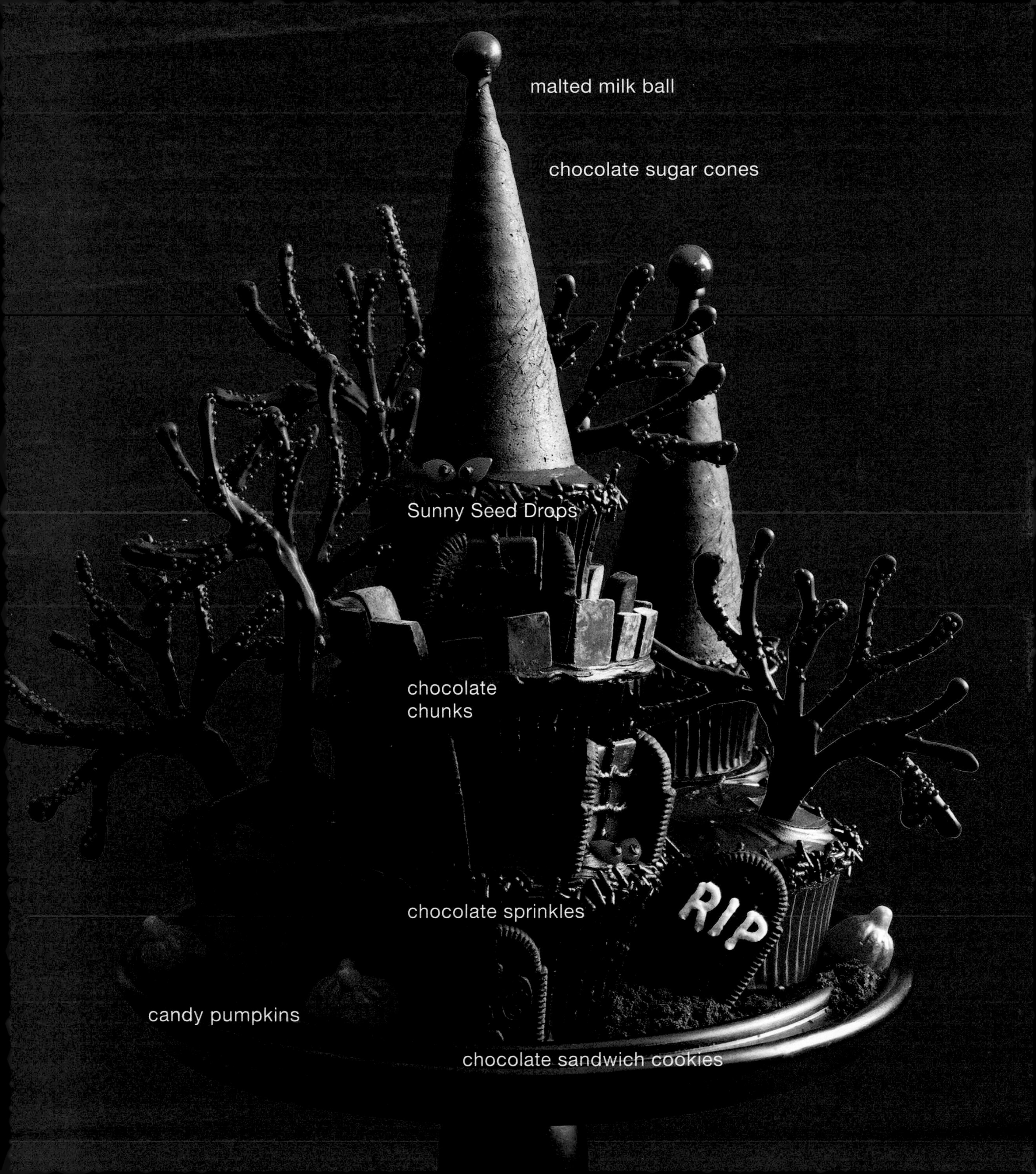

malted milk ball

chocolate sugar cones

Sunny Seed Drops

chocolate
chunks

chocolate sprinkles

RIP

candy pumpkins

chocolate sandwich cookies

THE HAUNTED HOUSE

Talk about curb appeal! Our haunted house is so pretty you won't want to eat it. But dive in, because almost every part is made from decadent dark chocolate: ice cream cones for the turrets, cookies for the shutters and door, candies for the finials and stones, and chocolate crumbs for the dirt.

2 **jumbo chocolate cupcakes baked in brown paper liners (see Sources)**

5 **chocolate cupcakes baked in brown paper liners (see Sources)**

2 **chocolate cupcakes baked in orange paper liners (see Sources)**

1 **cup dark cocoa candy melting wafers (Wilton)**

1 **tablespoon orange nonpareils (Cake Mate)**

2 **chocolate ice cream cones (Oreo)**

2 **round chocolate candies (chocolate-covered peanuts or malted milk balls)**

3 **oblong chocolate sandwich cookies (Oreo Dunkers, or cut an oblong shape from flat chocolate cookies)**

1 **tube (4.25 ounces) white decorating icing (Cake Mate)**

3 **chocolate chews (Tootsie Rolls)**

1 **can (16 ounces) dark chocolate frosting**

¼ **cup chocolate chunks (Saco Foods, Nestlé)**

1 **cup chocolate sprinkles**

4 **yellow candy-coated chocolate-covered sunflower seeds or chocolates (Sunny Seed Drops, M&M's Minis)**

½ **cup ground chocolate cookies (Oreos, Famous Chocolate Wafers; optional)**

Candy pumpkins (optional)

1. Place the tree template (page 156) on a cookie sheet and cover with wax paper. Place the dark cocoa melting wafers in a ziplock bag; do not seal the bag. Microwave for about 10 seconds to soften. Massage the mixture and return to the microwave. Repeat the process until the candy is smooth, about 1 minute total (see page 18). Press out the excess air and seal the bag.

2. Snip a small ($1/8$-inch) corner from the bag with the melted candy and follow the template to pipe a tree. Sprinkle the branches with the orange sprinkles while the candy is still wet (see page 18). Transfer the cookie sheet to the refrigerator for 5 minutes, or until firm. Repeat to make 6 trees. Pipe a dot of melted candy on the tip of each ice cream cone and add a round chocolate candy. Refrigerate until the melted candy is set, about 5 minutes.

3. Gently twist 2 of the chocolate sandwich cookies apart, using a paring knife to remove the filling. Use a serrated knife to cut each piece in half lengthwise. For the shutters and door, trim each halved piece to $1^{1}/_{2}$ inches in length. For the tombstone, pipe "RIP" with the white decorating icing on the remaining whole cookie. For the windows, roll the chocolate chews into rectangles and cut each into a $3/_{4}$-by-$1^{1}/_{4}$-inch piece.

4. Spoon $1/_{4}$ cup of the chocolate frosting into a ziplock bag, press out the excess air, seal, and set aside. Spread the top of 1 jumbo cupcake with some of the remaining chocolate frosting and smooth. Arrange the chocolate chunks all around the outer edge of the cupcake. Place the chocolate sprinkles in a small shallow bowl. Spread the tops of the remaining cupcakes with the remaining chocolate frosting and smooth. Roll the edges of the cupcakes in the chocolate sprinkles (see page 17).

5. For the tower, place the chocolate chunk–edged jumbo cupcake on top of the other jumbo cupcake. Place a standard cupcake in a brown paper liner on top of that in the center of the chocolate chunks. Add an ice cream cone, open end down, to make the turret. Place the tower on a cake stand or serving platter. Snip a small ($1/8$-inch) corner from the bag with the chocolate frosting. Pipe dots of chocolate frosting on the sides of the top and middle cupcakes and attach the chocolate chew rectangles as the windows (1 on the top; 2 on the middle). Pipe chocolate lines to make the panes and add the cookie shutters on either side. For the door, add a set of trimmed cookie halves at the base of the tower.

Place a cupcake in an orange liner on either side of the tower. Stack the 4 remaining cupcakes to make 2 smaller towers behind the central one.

6. Place the remaining chocolate cone on top of one of the shorter towers, open end down, to make a turret. Gently peel the chocolate trees from the wax paper and insert randomly on top of the back and side cupcakes (you can trim the bases to make shorter trees if necessary). Add 2 yellow candies side by side on the top and lower cupcakes of the central tower and pipe chocolate dots as the eyes. Sprinkle the chocolate cookie crumbs around the base of the structure as dirt, if using. Add the cookie tombstone and the candy pumpkins, if using.

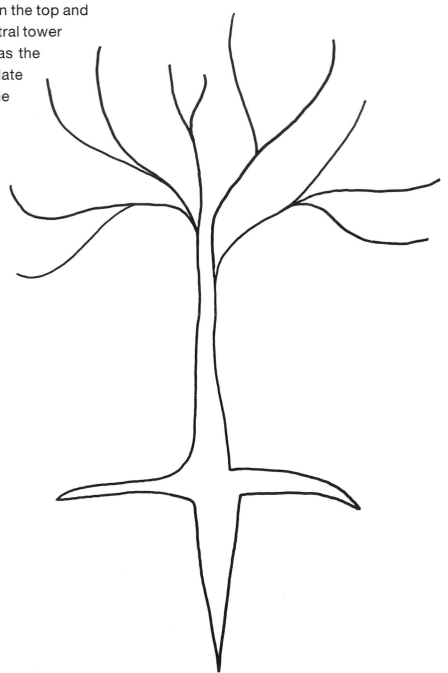

CHILLY GHOSTS

ez
CUPCAKE

Did you just feel a chill go through the house? Someone must have opened the freezer and let out the ghosts. Each chilly ghost cupcake has an ice cream center, and the ghosts are whipped topping piped from a ziplock bag. Ghosts keep well in the freezer until just before haunting time.

24 **chocolate cupcakes baked in brown paper liners (see Sources)**

1½ **cups ground chocolate cookies (Oreos, Famous Chocolate Wafers, chocolate graham crackers)**

1 **can (16 ounces) chocolate frosting**

2 **containers (8 ounces each) frozen whipped topping (Cool Whip), thawed in refrigerator**

24 **1½-inch balls of your favorite flavor ice cream**

48 **multicolored candy-coated chocolate-covered sunflower seeds or chocolates (Sunny Seed Drops, M&M's Minis)**

1. Using a paring knife, cut out a cone-shaped piece 1½ inches in diameter from the center of each cupcake and reserve for the top of the cupcake (see the photo on page 159).

2. Place the chocolate cookie crumbs in a small shallow bowl. Spread the chocolate frosting around the top of the cupcakes, leaving the opening unfrosted. Roll the tops in the cookie crumbs to cover (see page 17).

3. Divide the whipped topping between two ziplock bags. Snip a ³⁄₄-inch corner from each bag. Place the ice cream balls in the cupcake openings, pressing the ice cream down into the holes. Place the cone-shaped piece of cake on top, flat side down, and press down slightly (see the photo on page 159). Pipe a circle of the whipped topping around the base of the cone cake. Pipe a smaller circle on top of the ice cream and the whipped topping to cover the cake, then pipe a third layer of whipped topping, using a squeeze-release-pull motion (see page 13), to make the peaked ghost head.

4. Insert 2 matching candies for the eyes, pointed ends into the whipped topping. Serve immediately, or place in the freezer until ready to serve (if frozen, let the cupcakes stand at room temperature for 10 minutes before serving).

ALIEN INVASION

A close encounter of the cupcake kind. The design is eerie yet simple. The aliens are made from marshmallows and doughnut holes attached to standard-sized cupcakes. They are dipped in store-bought icing that's been colored bilious green and zapped in the microwave to liquefy it for dipping. Each creepy little alien sits in its own space capsule made from plastic take-out containers, allowing for easy transport to a party in the next galaxy.

24 vanilla cupcakes baked in silver foil liners (Reynolds)

 2 cans (16 ounces each) vanilla frosting

Neon green food coloring (McCormick)

12 marshmallows

24 plain doughnut holes

48 black candy-coated chocolate-covered sunflower seeds (Sunny Seed Drops)

Black licorice laces, cut into 1-inch pieces

24 plastic take-out containers (available at baking or party supply stores or see Sources)

1. Tint the vanilla frosting green with the food coloring. Using clean scissors, cut the marshmallows in half crosswise.

2. Spread a thin layer of the green frosting on top of the cupcakes and place 1 marshmallow half in the center of each cupcake, cut side down. Add a dot of frosting to the marshmallow and place a doughnut hole on top of the marshmallow, pressing it into the frosting. Spread frosting over the marshmallow and the doughnut hole to fill in the gaps and smooth (see page 14).

3. Place the assembled cupcakes on a cookie sheet in the freezer for 10 to 15 minutes, or until slightly frozen.

4. Working in batches, spoon $^3/_4$ cup of the remaining frosting into a 1-cup glass measuring cup. Microwave for 10- to 15-second intervals, stirring frequently, until the frosting is the consistency of lightly whipped cream.

5. Holding a chilled cupcake by its foil liner, dip it into the frosting right up to the edge of the liner. Hold the cupcake above the surface and allow the excess frosting to drip off (see page 15). Carefully turn the cupcake right side up and place on a cookie sheet. Repeat with the remaining cupcakes. When the frosting becomes too thick, reheat in the microwave for several seconds, stirring well. Add more frosting and reheat as necessary.

6. Press the black sunflower seeds onto the head area, pointed ends in, to make the eyes. Using a round toothpick, make 2 holes in the top of each alien and insert a piece of licorice in each hole for the antennae.

7. Carefully place each cupcake into a plastic container and top with the lid.

CREEPY CRAWLERS

In the mood to swallow a scorpion, bite a tick, or chew a centipede? Then this confectionery entomology is for you. The candy-coated chocolates and nuts used for the head, thorax, and abdomen of the creepy crawlers are glued together with chocolate. A specimen box purchased at a home-organization store is a cool idea for showcasing the cupcakes at a meeting of your local geek squad.

12 chocolate cupcakes baked in brown paper liners (see Sources)

Assortment of mini, regular, peanut butter, and almond candy-coated chocolates (a variety of M&M's)

Orange and brown candy-coated chocolate-covered sunflower seeds (Sunny Seed Drops)

1 cup dark cocoa melting wafers (Wilton)

1/2 cup peanut butter chips (Reese's)

1/2 cup coarse white decorating sugar (see Sources)

1 can (16 ounces) vanilla frosting

1. Separate the candies by color for each insect: yellow M&M's Peanut Butter and brown chocolate-covered sunflower seeds for the spider; green M&M's Minis and M&M's Almond for the beetle; red M&M's for the centipede; blue M&M's Peanut Butter and brown chocolate-covered sunflower seeds for the ticks; red M&M's Peanut Butter and M&M's Almond for the ant; and orange regular M&M's, M&M's Peanut Butter, chocolate-covered sunflower seeds, and peanut butter chips for the scorpion.

2. Place the 6 bug templates (page 166) on cookie sheets and cover with wax paper. Place the dark cocoa melting wafers in a ziplock bag. Do not seal the bag. Mi-

crowave for 10 seconds to soften. Massage the chocolate in the bag, return to the microwave, and repeat the process until the chocolate is smooth, about 1 minute total (see page 18). Press out the excess air and seal the bag.

3. Working on one bug template at a time (do not make the scorpion yet), snip a $1/16$-inch corner from the bag and pipe the legs and antennae on the wax paper. Pipe the body, making sure you connect all the chocolate parts. While the chocolate is still wet, add the candies (see photo). Continue with the remaining chocolate and candies, making 2 ants, 2 spiders, 6 ticks, 2 centipedes, and 2 beetles. Refrigerate until set, about 5 minutes.

4. Place the peanut butter chips in a ziplock bag. Do not seal the bag. Microwave for 10 seconds to soften. Massage the chips in the bag, return to the microwave, and repeat the process until the mixture is smooth, about 25 seconds total. Press out the excess air and seal the bag. For the scorpion, snip a $1/16$-inch corner from the bag and pipe the legs on the wax paper. Pipe the body and tail, making sure you connect all the parts. While the peanut butter mixture is still wet, add the orange candies. Make 2 scorpions. Refrigerate until set, about 5 minutes.

5. Place the white decorating sugar in a small shallow bowl. Spread the vanilla frosting on top of the cupcakes and smooth. Roll the edges of the cupcakes in the sugar (see page 17).

6. Carefully peel the hardened insects from the wax paper and transfer to the cupcakes, pressing down slightly into the frosting to secure. For the tick, place 3 ticks on each cupcake.

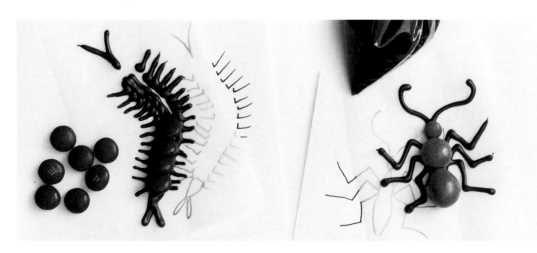

BUG TEMPLATES

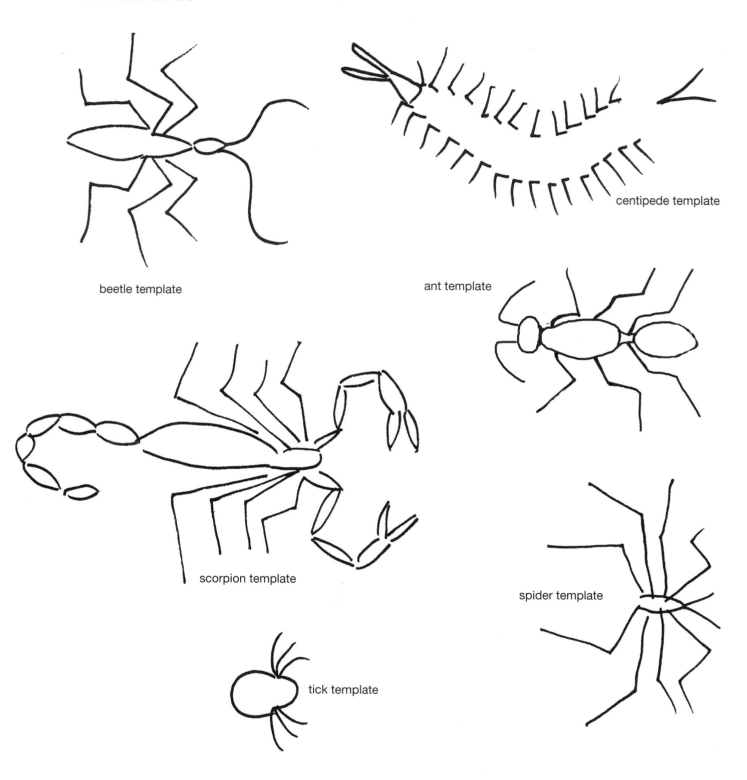

beetle template

centipede template

ant template

scorpion template

spider template

tick template

WHAT A HOOT!

CUPCAKE

Mama owl needs some really big eyes to watch out for her baby hooters, and making those big brown beauties is as easy as pulling apart an Oreo cookie. The pupils of Mama's eyes are Junior Mints and the babies' are M&M's. The beaks are yellow Runts and chocolate-covered sunflower seeds.

12 standard chocolate cupcakes baked in brown paper liners (see Sources)

24 mini chocolate cupcakes baked in brown paper liners (see Sources)

24 chocolate cream-filled sandwich cookies (Oreos)

48 mini chocolate cream-filled sandwich cookies (Mini Oreos)

2 tablespoons canned vanilla frosting

2 cans (16 ounces each) chocolate frosting

12 banana-shaped candies (Runts)

24 yellow candy-coated chocolate-covered sunflower seeds (Sunny Seed Drops)

24 mini chocolate-covered mints (Junior Mints)

48 brown mini candy-coated chocolates (M&M's Minis)

1. Microwave a few regular and mini cream-filled sandwich cookies at a time for several seconds (this will help keep the cream filling on one half when you separate the cookies). Be careful not to microwave the cookies for too long, or the filling will melt. Immediately twist each sandwich cookie apart so that you have a cream-covered side and a plain cookie side. Use a paring knife to remove any excess crumbs from the cream filling. Continue until all the cookies have been separated.

2. Using a serrated knife, make 2 parallel cuts ½ inch in from the edge on each regular plain cookie half. The 2 outside pieces with the rounded edges will be used for the ears on the mama owls. Cut the mini plain cookie halves in half.

3. Spoon the vanilla frosting and 1½ cups of the chocolate frosting into separate ziplock bags, press out the excess air, seal, and set aside. Spread the remaining chocolate frosting on top of the cupcakes and smooth.

4. Using a little chocolate frosting, attach 2 of the large ear pieces, rounded sides in and about 1½ inches apart, on top of each of the 12 standard cupcakes. Angle the ears slightly away from each other and allow them to extend about ¾ inch beyond the edge of the cupcake. Repeat the process with the mini cookies and the mini cupcakes, placing the ears about ½ inch apart and allowing a ½-inch overhang.

5. Place 2 regular cream-sided cookie halves, cream side up, on the upper half of each standard cupcake to make the eyes. Do the same with the mini cream-sided cookie halves and the mini cupcakes.

6. Snip a ⅛-inch corner from the bags with the chocolate and vanilla frosting. Pipe lines of chocolate frosting along the length of the cookie ears to cover. Starting with the edge at the top of the cupcake, pipe the feathers with the chocolate frosting using the squeeze-release-pull technique (see page 13). Work inward from the edge in slightly overlapping rows until the section above the eyes is covered. On the standard cupcakes, pipe a few feathers on the edge just below each eye. On the mini cupcakes, pipe several small feathers along the edge beside each eye.

7. Press a yellow candy in the middle of each cupcake to make the beak: the banana-shaped candies on the standard cupcakes, the candied sunflower seeds on the mini cupcakes. Use a dot of vanilla frosting on the cream of each cookie to attach a chocolate-covered mint to the eyes on the standard cupcakes and a brown chocolate candy to the eyes on the mini cupcakes. Place the eyes in different positions to give the owls character. Using the vanilla frosting, pipe a white highlight on each eye.

JACK-O'-LANTERNS

Who put the faux in the pumpkin glow? Yellow fruit chews, slightly smaller than the Tootsie Rolls underneath, let the light shine through. The pumpkins' ribs are piped from a ziplock bag, and the stems and split-rail fencing are crafted from pretzels.

6 jumbo Pumpkin-Spice Cupcakes (page 222) baked in orange paper liners (see Sources)

1 can (16 ounces) vanilla frosting

Orange food coloring (see Sources)

1/2 teaspoon unsweetened cocoa powder

16 chocolate chews (Tootsie Rolls)

16 yellow fruit chews (Tootsie Fruit Rolls, Starburst, Laffy Taffy)

3 wheat twist pretzels (Rold Gold)

1. Tint the vanilla frosting deep orange with the orange food coloring and cocoa powder. Divide the frosting between two ziplock bags, press out the excess air, and seal.

2. Soften several chocolate chews at a time in the microwave for 2 to 3 seconds. Roll out each chew on a piece of wax paper to a 1/8-inch thickness. Using the outer line of the templates (page 172), cut out shapes using a small paring knife or scissors. Reheat and reroll the scraps as necessary to make all of the templates. Repeat with the yellow fruit chews and the inner line of the templates.

3. Place the yellow pieces on top of the chocolate pieces to make the eyes, mouths, and noses; set aside on wax paper.

4. Snip a 1/4-inch corner from the bags with the orange frosting. Starting at the top of a cupcake, pipe a thick line of frosting down the center. To make the pumpkin's ribs, pipe vertical lines on either side of the center line, tapering them slightly at the top and bottom. Repeat with the remaining cupcakes.

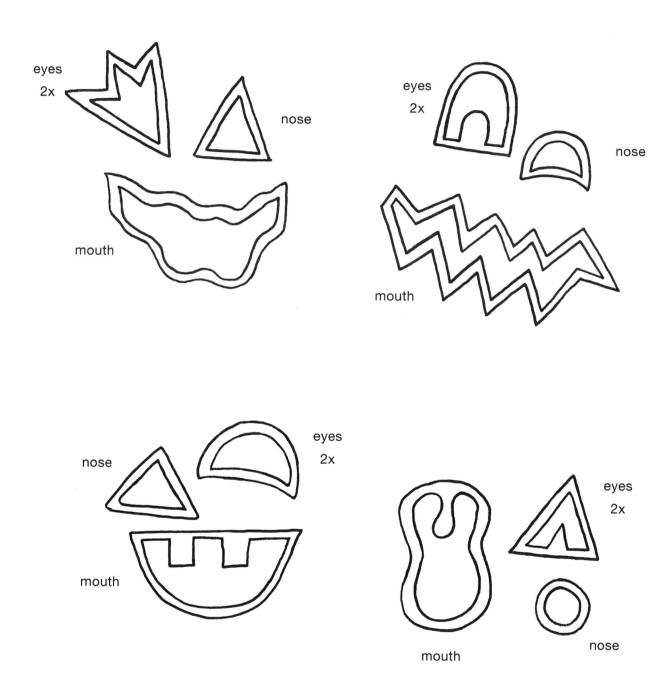

eyes
2x

nose

mouth

eyes
2x

nose

mouth

nose

eyes
2x

mouth

mouth

eyes
2x

nose

5. Arrange the face parts on top of the cupcakes (see the photo on page 171). For the stems, cut the wheat twist pretzels in half crosswise with a serrated knife and insert the cut ends into the top of the cupcakes.

PRETZEL FENCES

¹/₄ cup white chocolate chips

40 thin pretzel sticks (Rold Gold)

1. Line a cookie sheet with wax paper. Place the white chocolate chips in a ziplock bag; do not seal the bag. Microwave for about 10 seconds to soften. Massage the mixture and return to the microwave. Repeat the process until the chocolate is smooth, about 30 seconds total (see page 18). Press out the excess air and seal the bag.

2. Snip a small (¹/₈-inch) corner from the bag with the melted white chocolate. Place 2 thin pretzel sticks on the prepared cookie sheet about 2 inches apart. Pipe 2 dots of the melted white chocolate, at ³/₄-inch and 1¹/₂-inch intervals. Place 2 pretzel sticks crosswise, attaching at the chocolate dots to make a fence (see page 19). Repeat with the remaining pretzel sticks and white chocolate. Refrigerate until set, about 5 minutes. Arrange a few pretzel fences around the cupcakes on a serving platter.

MR. BONES JANGLE

We take the skeleton out of the closet and put it on the cupcakes. Mr. Jangle's white chocolate bones are easy to make ahead of time. On All Hallow's Eve, just frost the cupcakes and add the bones!

11 chocolate cupcakes baked in black paper liners (see Sources)

12 orange paper liners (see Sources)

1 black paper liner (see Sources)

1 cup white candy melting wafers (Wilton)

1¼ cups ground chocolate cookies (Oreos, Famous Chocolate Wafers)

1 cup canned chocolate frosting

Orange and black gummy worms or crunchy worms for garnish

1. Place the bone templates (page 176) on two cookie sheets. Cover with wax paper. Place the white candy melting wafers in a ziplock bag; do not seal the bag. Microwave for about 10 seconds to soften. Massage the mixture and return to the microwave. Repeat the process until the candy is smooth, about 1 minute (see page 18). Press out the excess air and seal.

2. Snip a small (⅛-inch) corner from the bag and, following the bone templates, pipe an outline. Fill in the bones with melted candy. Use a toothpick to pull the melted candy into the smaller areas. Tap the pans lightly to smooth the surface. Transfer the cookie sheets to the refrigerator for 5 minutes, or until firm.

3. Spoon the cookie crumbs into a small shallow bowl. Spread the frosting on top of the cupcakes and smooth. Roll the top of the cupcakes in the crumbs to cover completely (see page 17).

4. Place each cupcake in an orange paper liner. Arrange the cupcakes in a skeleton shape on a serving platter (see photo opposite page). Carefully peel the bones from the wax paper and place them on the cupcakes as shown, pressing them into the crumbs and frosting. Garnish with gummy worms in paper liners.

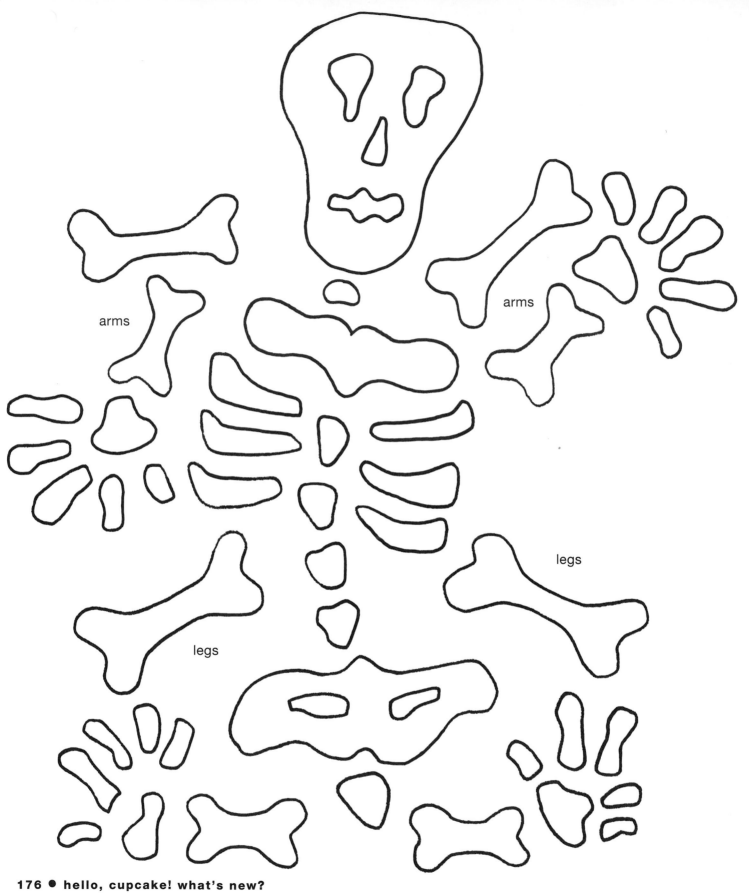

arms

arms

legs

legs

HOWLING WEREWOLVES

This pack of cupcakes will scare up a howling good time. Their fiery red fruit-leather mouths and neon candy eyes will send a chill down your spine. The snouts, cut from marshmallows, are shaped to bark, yelp, yap, and bay at the moon.

12 chocolate cupcakes baked in brown paper liners (see Sources)

¹/₂ cup canned vanilla frosting

1 cup canned dark chocolate frosting

Black food coloring (see Sources)

1 can (16 ounces) chocolate frosting

24 marshmallows

Red fruit leather (Fruit by the Foot)

8 each orange, yellow, and green candy-coated chocolates (M&M's)

12 black jelly beans (Jelly Belly)

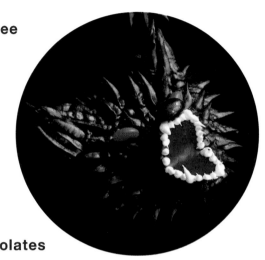

1. Spoon the vanilla frosting into a ziplock bag, press out the excess air, and seal. Tint the dark chocolate frosting black with the food coloring. Spoon half of the black frosting up one side of a ziplock bag. Spoon half of the chocolate frosting up the other side of the bag. Press out the excess air and seal the bag. Repeat the process with the remaining frosting in another ziplock bag. Press out the excess air and seal the bag.

2. To make the ears, lay 12 of the marshmallows on their sides and cut off both of the corners at one end, angling your knife so that the cut side will be about 1 inch wide. Use the remaining 12 marshmallows to make the muzzles by cutting a ¹/₂- to 1-inch V-shaped notch from the end of each marshmallow (see photo, page 178). The size of the notch will determine the size of the mouth.

3. Snip a ⅛-inch corner from one of the bags with the chocolate frosting. Pipe a small dot of frosting on the cut side of each ear and on the flat side of the muzzle. Attach the ears on either side at the top of each chocolate cupcake and place the muzzle just below the center. Cut 1- or 2-inch-long ovals from the red fruit leather to fit the notched mouth openings and press into the notches of the muzzles to stick. Trim off any excess fruit leather with clean scissors.

4. Working on one cupcake at a time, pipe several lines of chocolate frosting along the length of the ears to cover. Starting at the edge, pipe a ½-inch border around the cupcake using the squeeze-release-pull technique (see page 13), always pulling the frosting away from the center. Pipe another row inside the first, slightly overlapping the rows. Continue piping concentric rows of frosting, covering the cupcake and working your way up the marshmallow snout to the open mouth. Repeat with the remaining cupcakes and the second bag of chocolate frosting.

5. Press 2 chocolate candies of a matching color, edges in and at an angle, into the frosting to make the glowing eyes. Snip a ⅛-inch corner from the bag with the vanilla frosting and pipe sharp fangs all around the edge of the fruit leather, using the squeeze-release-pull technique (see page 13). Add a black jelly bean, crosswise, for the nose.

BLACK CATS

If a black cat crosses your path, it's your lucky day, especially if it's made from chocolate and coated in black sugar. The harvest moons underneath our kitties are cupcakes dipped in yellow frosting.

12 vanilla cupcakes baked in black paper liners (see Sources)

1 cup dark cocoa candy melting wafers (Wilton)

1 cup black decorating sugar (see Sources)

1 cup plus 2 tablespoons canned vanilla frosting

Yellow food coloring

1. Place a cat template (page 182) on a cookie sheet and cover with wax paper.

2. Place the cocoa candy melting wafers in a ziplock bag; do not seal the bag. Microwave for 10 seconds to soften. Massage and return to the microwave. Repeat the process until the candy is smooth, about 45 seconds total (see page 18). Press out the excess air and seal.

3. Snip a small (1/8-inch) corner from the bag and pipe the outline of the cat on the wax paper. Fill in the cat with the melted candy. Tap the pan lightly to smooth the surface. Sprinkle the top of the wet melted candy with the black sugar to cover. Repeat to make 13 cats (the extra one is in case of breakage). Refrigerate until set, about 5 minutes.

4. Tint the vanilla frosting bright yellow with the food coloring. Spoon 2 tablespoons of the yellow frosting into a small ziplock bag, press out the excess air, and seal.

5. Spoon the remaining yellow frosting into a shallow microwavable bowl. Heat the frosting in the microwave, stopping to stir frequently, until it has the texture of lightly whipped cream, 10 to 15 seconds.

6. Holding a cupcake by its paper liner, dip it into the frosting just up to the edge of the liner. Allow the excess frosting to drip off back into the bowl (see page 15). Carefully invert the cupcake and place on a cookie sheet. Repeat with the remaining cupcakes. If the frosting becomes too thick, microwave for several seconds, stirring well.

7. Snip a very small ($^1/_{16}$-inch) corner from the bag with the yellow frosting and pipe the slanted eyes on the cats. Snip a larger corner from the bag and pipe a dot of yellow frosting near one edge of each cupcake. Carefully peel the cats from the wax paper and place one on top of each cupcake, using the dot of frosting to secure.

LARRY THE TURKEY

Larry the Turkey does double duty at Thanksgiving, letting Larry know where to sit at the beginning of the meal and providing a dessert for him at the end. A delicious combination of pumpkin cupcakes, caramel frosting, and ginger cookies, this turkey will be gobbled up in no time. Of course, the best part is naming each turkey and hearing the kids scream, "Hey, look, everybody, Uncle Larry's a turkey!"

24 **standard Pumpkin-Spice cupcakes (page 222) baked in white paper liners**

24 **mini Pumpkin-Spice cupcakes (page 222) baked in white paper liners**

1 **cup canned vanilla frosting**

1/2 **cup canned chocolate frosting**

24 **thin ginger-flavored scalloped cookies (Anna's Ginger Thins)**

2 **cups candy corn**

1 1/2 **cups chocolate sprinkles (see Sources)**

1 **can (16 ounces) plus 1 cup caramel frosting**

24 **pieces Indian candy corn**

48 **brown candy-coated chocolate-covered sunflower seeds (Sunny Seed Drops)**

1 **roll red fruit leather (Fruit by the Foot)**

24 **graham cracker sticks (Honey Maid Graham Sticks)**

12 **marshmallows**

1. Spoon the vanilla and chocolate frosting into separate ziplock bags, press out the excess air, and seal. Snip a $\frac{1}{8}$-inch corner from the bag with the vanilla frosting and pipe a dot of frosting on 7 adjacent scallops on each ginger cookie to make the tail fan. Add a piece of candy corn to each dot of frosting, pointed end facing in (see photo, opposite page).

2. Place the chocolate sprinkles in a small shallow bowl. Spread the caramel frosting on top of all the cupcakes, standard and mini, and smooth. Roll the edge of the standard cupcakes in the sprinkles (see page 17). Dip the top edge of the mini cupcakes in the sprinkles. Using clean scissors, cut the marshmallows in half on the diagonal. Place 1 marshmallow half, cut side down, near the edge of one of the standard cupcakes, with the tapered end facing the center, to make a support for the tail.

3. Press 1 piece of Indian candy corn into the center of each mini cupcake, flat side down, for the beak. Pipe 2 dots of the vanilla frosting above the beak for the eyes and insert 2 brown candied sunflower seeds, pointed end down. Cut the red fruit leather into twenty-four $1\frac{1}{2}$-inch-long teardrop shapes and lay them over the beak to make the wattle.

4. Snip a $\frac{1}{8}$-inch corner from the bag with the chocolate frosting and pipe names on the flat side of the graham cracker sticks. Reserve the bag for final assembly. Cupcakes may be made up to this point several hours in advance.

5. When ready to assemble (no more than 2 hours in advance), enlarge the hole in the corner of the bag with the chocolate frosting to $\frac{1}{4}$ inch. Pipe a dot of chocolate frosting on the tapered end of the marshmallow. Place the tail cookie on the marshmallow, pressing the undecorated edge into the frosting on the marshmallow. Add the mini cupcake head on top so that half of it is resting on the undecorated edge of the cookie and the other half is pressed lightly into the frosting to secure.

6. Add the graham crackers at the base of the mini cupcakes, securing with a dot of frosting.

7. Arrange the turkeys on the table as place cards. Place 2 candy corns on the table in front of each turkey to make the feet.

Hooray for Holly Days

Hooray for holly days, where edible ornaments are a cupcake craze, blue poinsettias are all the rage, and punch-drunk elves act in wacky ways. A festive time when polar bears can float on cupcakes without a care, trees grow chocolate needles and candy stars too, and gingerbread boys say, "Happy holidays to you."

Eye-Candy Ornaments   188

Edible Ornaments   190

Gingerbread Boys   193

Punch-Drunk Elves   196

Blue Poinsettias   200

Frosty Mugs   202

Oh Tannenbaum   204

Polar Bears   208

White Wreath   211

Gingerbread Village   214

decorating sugar

sugar cookie dough

EYE-CANDY ORNAMENTS

As colorful as stained glass on a cupcake, these ornaments are created from store-bought cookie dough baked with crushed hard candies in the center. They are so pretty that you may want to bake extra for your tree.

12 vanilla cupcakes baked in silver foil liners (Reynolds)

1 recipe dough from Quick Sugar Cookies (page 225)

12 thin pretzel sticks (Bachman)

$3/4$ cup each red, green, and blue crushed hard candies (Jolly Rancher)

$1/3$ cup each blue, green, red, and yellow decorating sugars (see Sources)

$1/3$ cup light corn syrup

1 can (16 ounces) vanilla frosting

Yellow food coloring

$3/4$ cup coarse white decorating sugar (see Sources)

1. Preheat the oven to 350°F and line two cookie sheets with parchment paper. Using the template (opposite page) or a homemade cookie cutter made from the template, cut the rolled-out cookie dough into 12 ornament shapes following the directions on page 20. Transfer the cutouts to the prepared pans, spacing about 1 inch apart. Cut out the centers of the ornaments with a small paring knife, lid, or round cookie cutter, removing a $1^{1}/_{2}$-inch circle from each. Use a straw to make a small hole at the top of the ornament. Press a pretzel stick into the cookie dough at the base of the cookie cutouts to form the support for the ornament (see page 19); the placement of the pretzels should be varied to give the finished ornaments a tumbled look.

2. Bake the cookies until just golden and firm to the touch, 7 to 10 minutes. Transfer the pans to wire racks. Spoon about 2 tablespoons of the crushed candies (keeping the colors separate) in the center of each cookie cutout. Return the pans to the oven and bake until the candies are just melted and smooth on top, about 2 minutes (see page 21). Transfer the pans to the wire racks and allow to cool completely.

3. Carefully peel the candy-filled cookies from the parchment paper. Place the blue, green, and red decorating sugars in separate shallow bowls. Heat the corn syrup in the microwave until bubbly, 8 to 10 seconds. Working on 1 cookie at a time and using a small brush, lightly paint corn syrup on the smooth side of the circular cookie surface. Dip the cookie into the matching colored sugar to coat. Brush off the excess sugar from the candy area with a dry brush. Repeat with the remaining cookies and sugars.

4. Tint ½ cup of the vanilla frosting yellow with the food coloring. Spoon the yellow frosting into a ziplock bag, press out the excess air, and seal. Snip a small (⅛-inch) corner from the bag and pipe decorative lines at the top of the ornament to make the hanger. Sprinkle the frosted area with the yellow decorating sugar.

5. Place the coarse white decorating sugar in a small shallow bowl. Frost the tops of the cupcakes with the remaining vanilla frosting and swirl. Roll the edge of the frosted cupcakes in the sugar (see page 17). Arrange the cupcakes on a serving platter. Just before serving, insert the ornaments' pretzel sticks into the tops of the cupcakes.

EDIBLE ORNAMENTS

These ornaments are a press-and-play project: there's nothing more to it than pressing candies into the frosting. No piping fancy designs, no complicated shaping, and nothing to melt. Simply frost the cupcakes, roll them in sugar, choose colorful and graphic candies, and press them into your own beautiful designs. Make a batch for a holiday dessert or put them in mini gift boxes for a sweet party favor or take-along gift.

8 vanilla cupcakes baked in red paper liners (see Sources)

8 vanilla cupcakes baked in green paper liners (see Sources)

8 vanilla cupcakes baked in white paper liners

2 cans (16 ounces each) vanilla frosting

1/2 cup each green, light green, red, yellow, and white decorating sugars (see Sources)

24 yellow spice drops

Black licorice laces, cut into twenty-four 1 1/4-inch pieces

24 thin pretzel sticks (Bachman)

Assortment of colored fruit chews and fruit leather (Laffy Taffy, Airheads, Starburst, Fruit by the Foot)

Red licorice laces

1 cup mini candy-coated chocolates (M&M's Minis)

Small red cinnamon candies (Red Hots) or candy decors

1. Spoon 1/2 cup of the vanilla frosting into a ziplock bag, press out the excess air, seal, and set aside.

2. Place the decorating sugars in separate small shallow bowls. Spread the tops of all the cupcakes with the vanilla frosting, mounding it slightly. Starting at the edge, roll the top of each cupcake in one of the sugars to coat completely (see page 17).

3. To make the top of the ornament, use a round toothpick to poke a hole in each end of one of the spice drops. Bend one of the black licorice pieces in half and insert both ends into the hole in the bottom of the spice drop to make a loop. Insert one end of a pretzel stick into the hole in the rounded top of the spice drop, pushing it in about $\frac{1}{2}$ inch. Press the other end of the pretzel all the way into one of the cupcakes. Repeat with the remaining cupcakes.

4. Roll out the fruit chews on a piece of wax paper to $\frac{1}{8}$ inch thick. Use a pastry wheel, clean craft scissors, or regular scissors to cut the fruit chews and fruit leather into decorative pieces. Arrange the fruit-chew pieces, fruit leather, and red laces on top of the cupcakes to make stripes, bands, and lines. Snip a $\frac{1}{8}$-inch corner from the bag with the vanilla frosting and pipe dots in different patterns over the cupcakes and on top of the fruit chews. Press the chocolate candies, Cinnamon Red Hots, and candy decors into the frosting to secure.

5. Set the cupcakes in another paper liner and place in small boxes or on a serving platter.

GINGERBREAD BOYS

CUPCAKE

Gingerbread and chocolate are two of our favorite things, so what could be better than combining them in these delicious gingerbread boys? Our Next-to-Instant Ganache (page 224), made by zapping store-bought icing in the microwave, produces the sophisticated candy-coated sheen. It may take a little practice to bridge the gaps between the cupcakes with the white-frosting outline, but if the line breaks, just go back and start piping again. The still-soft frosting will melt into itself and heal the break.

21 Gingerbread or Orange-Spice cupcakes (page 222) baked in brown paper liners (see Sources)

1 cup canned vanilla frosting

1 can (16 ounces) milk chocolate frosting

3 each red, green, and yellow spice drops

6 green candy-coated chocolates (M&M's)

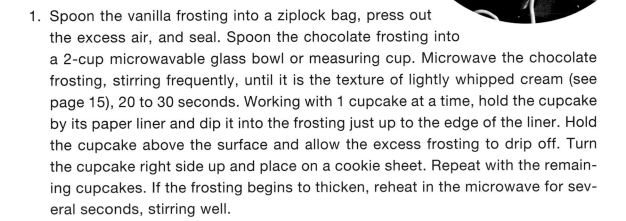

1. Spoon the vanilla frosting into a ziplock bag, press out the excess air, and seal. Spoon the chocolate frosting into a 2-cup microwavable glass bowl or measuring cup. Microwave the chocolate frosting, stirring frequently, until it is the texture of lightly whipped cream (see page 15), 20 to 30 seconds. Working with 1 cupcake at a time, hold the cupcake by its paper liner and dip it into the frosting just up to the edge of the liner. Hold the cupcake above the surface and allow the excess frosting to drip off. Turn the cupcake right side up and place on a cookie sheet. Repeat with the remaining cupcakes. If the frosting begins to thicken, reheat in the microwave for several seconds, stirring well.

2. Arrange 7 cupcakes on a serving platter or cookie sheet to make a gingerbread boy, making sure the cupcakes lightly touch one another: 3 cupcakes in a vertical row for the head and body, 2 on either side of the bottom cupcake for the feet, and 2 on either side of the second cupcake for the hands (see photo, opposite page). Repeat to make 2 more gingerbread boys.

3. Snip a ⅛-inch corner from the bag with the vanilla frosting. Pipe an outline of the gingerbread boy along the outer edge of each cupcake group using the "flying"-line technique (page 13). Pipe 3 dots of vanilla frosting down the center of the body and add the spice drops to make the buttons. Pipe 2 dots for the eyes and add the green chocolate candies. Pipe a mouth.

PUNCH-DRUNK ELVES

Goofy, Loopy, Droopy, Sloppy, and Punch. How'd they get so drunk? We spiked the cake with rum flavor. Their hats are custom-cut cookies; pretzels on the back hold them in place. The taffy ears and jelly bean noses flush pink from all that booze.

12 **Spice-Rum Cupcakes (page 221) baked in green paper liners (see Sources)**

 1 **recipe dough from Quick Sugar Cookies (page 225) or 12 whole rectangular graham crackers**

³/₄ cup white chocolate chips

36 **thin pretzel sticks (Bachman)**

 6 **green fruit chews (Jolly Rancher, Laffy Taffy)**

 6 **pink fruit chews (Starburst, Jolly Rancher, Laffy Taffy)**

 1 **can (16 ounces) vanilla frosting**

Green and red food coloring

³/₄ cup green decorating sugar (see Sources)

12 **yellow candy-coated chocolates (M&M's)**

 1 **tube (4.25 ounces) chocolate decorating icing (Cake Mate)**

12 **small light pink jelly beans (Jelly Belly)**

Granulated sugar to support cupcakes (optional)

Punch cups (optional)

1. If using the cookie dough, preheat the oven to 350°F and line two cookie sheets with parchment paper. Roll out the dough following the directions on page 225 and cut 12 hat shapes using the template on page 198. Bake the cookies until just golden and firm to the touch, 7 to 10 minutes. Transfer to a wire rack and allow to cool completely.

2. If using graham crackers, cut them in half crosswise with a small serrated knife.

Follow the template to cut a tall triangle from each (see photo, opposite page). Reserve the tall triangle and 1 trimmed piece to make the elf hats. Line two cookie sheets with wax paper. Arrange the larger graham pieces on the wax paper. Place the smaller graham pieces next to the larger grahams, near the top edge to make the hat shape.

3. Place the white chocolate chips in a ziplock bag; do not seal the bag. Microwave for about 10 seconds to soften. Massage the mixture and return to the microwave. Repeat the process until the white chocolate is smooth, about 30 seconds (see page 18). Press out the excess air and seal. Snip a small ($\frac{1}{8}$-inch) corner from the bag and pipe a line along the short end of the smaller cracker piece. Attach to the side of the larger cracker to make the hat. Repeat with the remaining crackers.

4. Pipe some white chocolate in the center of the cookie or cracker hat and place 2 pretzel sticks side by side $\frac{3}{4}$ inch apart in the melted chocolate, allowing them to overhang the wide bottom edge by about 2 inches. Use an extra pretzel stick to support the overhanging pretzels while they harden (see photo, opposite page). Repeat with the remaining pretzel sticks. Refrigerate until set, about 5 minutes.

5. Roll out each green fruit chew on a clean work surface to a 1-by-1$\frac{1}{2}$-inch rectangle. For the hat brims, cut each rectangle in half lengthwise. Roll out the pink fruit chews to a $\frac{1}{8}$-inch thickness. For the ears, cut the pink chews into twenty-four 1-inch ovals. Pinch the short ends to form the ears.

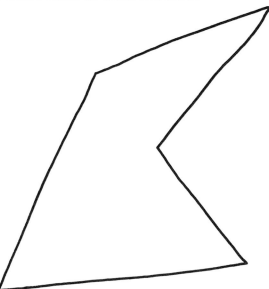

5. Tint ¾ cup of the vanilla frosting green with the food coloring. Place the green sugar in a small shallow bowl. Spread a thin layer of the green frosting on the flat side of a hat assembly. Dip the frosted side into the green sugar to coat. Repeat with the remaining hats. Spread a small line of green frosting on the bottom edge of the hats and add the green fruit chew brims, trimming the ends to fit. Attach the yellow candy at the tip of the hat with a dot of green frosting.

6. Tint 3 tablespoons of the vanilla frosting red with the red food coloring. Spoon the red frosting into a small ziplock bag. Spoon 3 tablespoons of the vanilla frosting into a small ziplock bag. Press out the excess air and seal the bags.

7. Tint the remaining vanilla frosting light pink with a drop or two of red food coloring. Spread the pink frosting on top of the cupcakes and smooth. Insert the pretzel ends of the hat assembly at one edge of the cupcake to secure. Snip a very small corner from each bag, with the red and white frosting. For open eyes, pipe 2 white dots; add a dot of chocolate decorating icing for the pupil. For closed or squinty eyes, pipe lines of decorating icing. Add a pink jelly bean, crosswise, for the nose. Pipe a squiggled red line as the mouth. Add the fruit chew for the ears. Spoon sugar into punch cups, if using, and add the cupcakes.

BLUE POINSETTIAS

CUPCAKE

We'd sing "Blue Christmas" except that these poinsettias are too festive to be sad and too easy to save just for Christmas. We cut the petals from frosty blue Wintermint gum and placed them on cupcakes frosted in white. For a more traditional look, use Big Red gum and red paper liners.

12 vanilla cupcakes baked in blue paper liners (see Sources)

90 sticks blue gum (Wrigley's Orbit Wintermint)

1 cup coarse white decorating sugar (see Sources)

1¹/₂ cups canned vanilla frosting

36 yellow mini candy-coated chocolates (M&M's Minis)

1. Working in small batches so the gum doesn't dry out before it is shaped, unwrap a few pieces at a time and cut with a clean pair of scissors following the petal templates at right. Gently pinch the flat end to make 60 large and 60 small petals. Allow the gum to dry for 30 minutes before assembling.

2. Place the white decorating sugar in a small shallow bowl. Spread the tops of the cupcakes with the vanilla frosting and smooth. Roll the edges of the cupcakes in the sugar (see page 17).

3. Arrange 10 to 12 petals of various sizes on top of each cupcake, inserting the pinched end of the gum slices in the center of the cupcake. Add 3 yellow candies in the center to make the poinsettias. Arrange the poinsettia cupcakes on a serving platter to make a wreath.

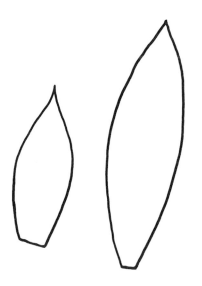

FROSTY MUGS

We gave our snowmen a fresh face, rolling the frosting in sugar for extra sparkle. We added chocolate morsels for eyes, mini morsels for mouths, and orange fruit slices for carrot noses. The magic in the top hat comes from a chocolate wafer cookie.

24 **chocolate cupcakes baked in silver foil liners (Reynolds)**

1¼ **cups coarse white decorating sugar (see Sources)**

24 **thin chocolate cookies (Famous Chocolate Wafers)**

12 **orange candy fruit slices**

2 **cans (16 ounces each) vanilla frosting**

Green food coloring

¼ **cup chocolate chips**

¼ **cup mini chocolate chips**

Large red sprinkles (see Sources)

1. Place the white decorating sugar in a small shallow bowl. For the hats, using a serrated knife and angling it slightly inward from top to bottom, cut ¼ inch from opposite sides of the chocolate cookies. Reserve 24 of the smaller cookie pieces for the hat brims. For the noses, cut each orange fruit slice into two ¼-by-³⁄₄-by-³⁄₄-inch triangles.

2. Tint ¼ cup of the frosting green with the food coloring. Spoon the green frosting into a small ziplock bag, press out the excess air, and seal. Spread the remaining vanilla frosting on top of the cupcakes, mounding it slightly. Roll the tops in the decorating sugar to cover completely (see page 17).

3. Press the base of an orange candy nose into the center of each cupcake. Add the standard chocolate chips, pointed ends down, for the eyes. Add the mini chocolate chips, pointed ends down, as the mouth.

4. Right before serving, use a small paring knife to cut a slit in each cupcake, parallel to the edge. Insert the large cookie piece, small end in, as the hat. Add a smaller cookie piece, cut edge down, as the brim. Snip a small (1/8-inch) corner from the bag with the green frosting and pipe a decorative edge along the crown of the hat or pipe a few holly leaves and add a couple of red sprinkles.

OH TANNENBAUM

The long needles of our stunning pine centerpiece are green candy wafers drizzled from a ziplock bag. The star is crafted from melted hard candies.

24 vanilla cupcakes baked in green paper liners (see Sources)

1 cup green candy melting wafers (Wilton)

1 can (16 ounces) vanilla frosting

Green food coloring

2 tablespoons white nonpareils, plus more for the platters (see Sources)

¼ cup red mini candy-coated chocolates (M&M's Minis) or small red cinnamon candies (Red Hots)

1 red candy star (page 206)

1. Line three cookie sheets with wax paper. Place the green candy melting wafers in a ziplock bag; do not seal the bag. Microwave for about 10 seconds to soften. Massage the mixture and return to the microwave. Repeat the process until the candy is smooth, about 1 minute total. Press out the excess air and seal the bag. Snip a small (⅛-inch) corner from the bag and pipe a continuous tight zig-zag row, about 2½ inches wide and close together, down the length of a cookie sheet (see page 18). Make 2 more rows. Repeat to fill the remaining 2 cookie sheets. Refrigerate until set, about 5 minutes.

2. Tint the vanilla frosting green with the food coloring. Spread the tops of 4 cup-cakes with green frosting, mounding it slightly in the center. Break the green candy zigzags into smaller pieces to look like pine needles. Place on top of the cupcakes, allowing the pine needles to overhang slightly. Add white nonpareils and a few red candies. Repeat with the remaining cupcakes, frosting, and candy.

3. Arrange cupcakes around the perimeter of a square platter. Arrange more cup-cakes around the perimeter of a smaller square platter. Arrange 4 cupcakes close together on a small square plate. Set 1 cupcake on top, in the center of the 4 cupcakes. Add the red candy star in the center of the top cupcake, press-

ing into frosting to secure. Place small inverted glasses (tall enough to provide clearance for the cupcakes and needles) in the centers of the two larger platters, spaced to support the platter above. Place the middle-size platter on top of the glasses on the largest platter, and top off with the small plate with the star on top. Place any leftover cupcakes on small plates, positioning them around the tree. Add additional white nonpareils to the platters.

HOLIDAY'S BRIGHTEST STARS

Colorful candy stars make beautiful tree toppers. You can also make Hanukkah cupcakes by putting the stars on vanilla-frosted cupcakes baked in silver foil liners.

Hard candies: 4 red for the Christmas star; 40 blue for the Hanukkah stars (Jolly Rancher)

Metal star-shaped cookie cutters: one 2- to 3-inch five-pointed star cutter for the Christmas star; several six-pointed star cutters in a range of sizes from 1 to 3 inches for the Hanukkah stars

Vegetable cooking spray

1. Preheat the oven to 350°F. Line several cookie sheets with foil. Place the unwrapped hard candies in a ziplock bag; do not seal. Using a small hammer or the back of a saucepan, break the candies into small pieces. Sprinkle the candies in an even layer in the center of the prepared cookie sheets (see page 21).

2. Spray the cookie cutters with the vegetable cooking spray. Bake one cookie sheet at a time until the candies are just melted and smooth, 3 to 4 minutes. Transfer the cookie sheet to a wire rack. Immediately press the oiled cookie cutters, as close together as possible, into the melted candy. Let stand until the candy has cooled completely, about 5 minutes. Carefully break apart the candy sheet to remove the cutters and candy stars, reusing the candy scraps to break up for the next batch. Repeat with the other cookie sheets.

POLAR BEARS

Don't let anyone tell you polar bears aren't sweet because this one, covered in coconut-fur, is the tastiest we have ever met. This adorable guy lolls around on his back, holding his doughnut hole head and cute spice drop paws up in the air.

12 **vanilla cupcakes baked in white paper liners**

 1 **can (16 ounces) vanilla frosting**

¹/₂ **cup canned chocolate frosting**

12 **plain doughnut holes**

 1 **cup flaked sweetened coconut**

60 **white spice drops**

24 **frosted oat cereal O's (Frosted Cheerios)**

12 **brown mini candy-coated chocolates (M&M's Minis)**

Blue and white rock candy for garnish (optional)

1. Spoon ¹/₂ cup of the vanilla frosting into a ziplock bag. Spoon the chocolate frosting into a ziplock bag. Press out the excess air and seal the bags. Spread the top of the cupcakes with some of the remaining vanilla frosting, mounding it slightly. Place a doughnut hole close to one edge of each frosted cupcake. Place the cupcakes in the freezer until firm, 15 to 20 minutes.

2. Pulse the coconut in a food processor until finely chopped or chop by hand with a knife. Place the coconut in a small shallow bowl.

3. Spread the remaining vanilla frosting in a thin layer over the doughnut hole and fill in the gap around the base to smooth (see photo, page 210). Roll the assembled cupcake in the chopped coconut to cover completely (see page 17). Repeat with the remaining cupcakes.

4. Snip a small (¹/₈-inch) corner from the bags with the vanilla and chocolate frostings. For the bottom paws, flatten 24 of the spice drops lengthwise. For each

cupcake, pipe dots of vanilla frosting on top of the coated doughnut hole and attach the cereal pieces as the ears. Pipe a line of vanilla frosting around the ears and coat with coconut. Pipe dots of vanilla frosting on the cupcake and attach 2 of the flattened spice drops as the bottom paws. Pipe dots of vanilla frosting and attach the flat side of spice drops as the muzzle on the doughnut hole and the front paws on the cupcake. Pipe the mouth, eyes, claws (using the squeeze-release-pull technique, page 13), and pads on the spice drops using the chocolate frosting. Add the brown candy as the nose.

WHITE WREATH

This elegant holiday wreath will have your guests dreaming of a white Christmas. It is created using melting wafers painted on mint leaves. You can add even more winter freshness by decorating your wreath with crushed peppermint sticks. The holly berries are candy-coated chocolates, but any round red candy of the appropriate size will work. Adjust the size of the wreath to match your party, and if you have extra cupcakes, cover them with additional white chocolate leaves and red candies and place them around the table as decorations.

12 vanilla cupcakes baked in silver foil liners (Reynolds)

2 bunches fresh mint, preferably with large leaves

1¹/₂ cups white chocolate melting wafers (Wilton)

1 can (16 ounces) vanilla frosting

1 cup coarse white decorating sugar (see Sources)

1 cup red candy-coated milk chocolate balls (Cadbury)

1 decorative ribbon

1. Line 2 cookie sheets with wax paper. Pick the mint leaves from the stems. Wash and pat dry on paper towels.

2. Place the white chocolate melting wafers in a medium microwavable bowl. Microwave, stirring frequently, until the chocolate is smooth, about 1 minute.

3. Using a small, clean craft brush or your fingertip, coat the top side of each mint leaf with an even layer of the melted chocolate (see photo on page 212). Transfer to one of the cookie sheets, chocolate side up, and allow the leaf to bend and curve slightly. Repeat with the remaining mint leaves to make about 75 leaves. If the chocolate becomes too thick, reheat in the microwave for several seconds, stirring well. Place the leaves in the refrigerator until set, about 5 minutes.

4. Carefully peel the leaves from the hardened chocolate. They come off surprisingly easily. Use a toothpick or clean tweezers to remove any small pieces of mint leaf that may remain. (The leaves can be made up to 5 days in advance, covered, and kept in a cool dry place.)

5. Spoon ¼ cup of the vanilla frosting into a ziplock bag, press out the excess air, and seal. Spoon the decorating sugar into a small shallow bowl. Spread the tops of the cupcakes with the remaining vanilla frosting and smooth. Roll the edges of the cupcakes in the sugar (see page 17). Arrange the cupcakes, close together, in a circle on a large platter.

6. Press the white chocolate leaves into the cupcakes oriented in one direction to cover the cupcakes. Snip a ⅛-inch corner from the bag with the vanilla frosting and pipe dots of frosting randomly on the leaves to attach the red candies. Sprinkle the platter with the remaining decorative sugar. Tie a decorative ribbon into a bow and place on the platter.

GINGERBREAD VILLAGE

Anything you can do with a gingerbread house, we can do better with cupcakes. We turn our jumbo cupcakes (gingerbread, of course) on their sides and attach cookie bases and graham cracker roofs. You can make candy doors, cereal shingles, spice drop trees, and frosting icicles. Some of our favorite decorations are M&M's, red Twizzlers Pull-n-Peel licorice, white and yellow gum squares, chocolate-covered raisins, starlight mints, green Froot Loops, white jelly beans, snowflake sprinkles, red sour balls, thin pretzel sticks, red fruit leather, red sprinkles, Tootsie Rolls, Golden Grahams and Chex cereal, chocolate Sno-Caps, and flaked sweetened coconut — but use whatever you like. Welcome to your new holiday tradition.

5 jumbo Gingerbread Cupcakes (page 222) baked in brown paper liners (see Sources)

1 can (16 ounces) plus 1 cup vanilla frosting

Red, green, and brown food coloring (see Sources)

1 cup canned dark chocolate frosting

2 each red, green, yellow, and orange spice drops

3 tablespoons granulated sugar

5 whole graham crackers

2 vanilla creme wafers

5 marshmallows and/or candy spearmint leaves (Farley)

7 dark chocolate nonpareil candies (Sno-Caps)

Assorted candies and snacks for decorating (see headnote)

1. Tint ¼ cup of the vanilla frosting red with the food coloring. Tint ½ cup of the vanilla frosting green with the food coloring. Spoon 1 cup of the vanilla frost-

ing into a ziplock bag. Spoon the red, green, and dark chocolate frostings into separate ziplock bags. Press out the excess air and seal the bags. Tint the remaining vanilla frosting light brown with the brown food coloring and spoon into a ziplock bag. Keep the frosting covered until ready to use.

2. For the doors, press 2 like-colored spice drops together and roll out on a work surface sprinkled with the granulated sugar to a $1/8$-inch thickness. Cut the flattened gumdrops into doors measuring about $3/4$ by $1^1/2$ inches; cut off the top corners to create the rounded door.

3. For the house bases and roof pieces, using a serrated knife, cut 2 whole graham crackers, following the perforated lines, into 4 equal pieces each. Discard 1 piece; you will have 7 pieces. Cut the remaining 3 graham crackers into 6 pieces measuring 2 by $2^1/2$ inches. For one of the roofs, cut $3/4$ inch on the diagonal from one short end of each of the 2 vanilla creme wafers.

4. Snip a small ($1/8$-inch) corner from each bag of frosting. Spread the top of the cupcakes with the light brown frosting. Add a flattened gumdrop door to 4 of the cupcakes.

5. Using frostings for the glue, pipe decorations and attach assorted candies to outline doors, make windows and rock walls, and create anything else you want on the façade of your house. Use pretzel sticks to make timbers (see photo, page 214).

6. Cut the marshmallow and/or spearmint leaves in half on the diagonal. Place a quartered piece of graham cracker on a small plate or platter. Pipe a dot of vanilla frosting in the center of the graham cracker. Place the front edge of a decorated cupcake on its side on top of the cracker. Use the cut marshmallows and/or spearmint leaves, cut side down, on either side of the cupcake as support. Pipe some of the light brown frosting along the top edge of each cupcake. For the roofs, add the 6 larger graham cracker pieces to 3 of the cupcakes, the chocolate nonpareil candies to 1 cupcake, and the vanilla creme wafers to the remaining cupcake, using the remaining quarter graham cracker pieces behind as supports.

7. Using frostings for the glue, add shingles, pipe icicles (using the squeeze-release-pull technique, page 13), and attach assorted candies or whatever else inspires you.

SNOW-COVERED TREES

6 mini vanilla cupcakes baked in white paper liners

5 vanilla cupcakes baked in white paper liners

1 can (16 ounces) vanilla frosting

6 white spice drops

2 tablespoons white nonpareils (see Sources)

2 tablespoons coarse white decorating sugar (see Sources)

1. Divide the vanilla frosting between two ziplock bags, press out the excess air, and seal. Snip a small (1/8-inch) corner from each bag. Remove the paper liners from 5 of the mini cupcakes. Pipe a dot of frosting on top of the standard cupcakes and add the unwrapped mini cupcakes, top side down, pressing into the frosting. Pipe a dot in the center of each upside-down mini cupcake and press a spice drop, flat side down, into the frosting. Pipe a dot of frosting in the center of the mini cupcake with the liner and press a spice drop flat side down into the frosting to make a mini tree. Pipe the vanilla frosting around the edge of each cupcake using the squeeze-release-pull technique (see page 13), and then work upward in concentric circles, always pulling the frosting away from the center and slightly overlapping the rows, until the cupcake and spice drop are completely covered. Repeat with the remaining cupcakes.

2. Sprinkle the tops of the frosted cupcakes with the white nonpareils and decorating sugar.

Cupcakes, Frostings, and Cookies

Like most folks, we're busy, and we definitely don't want to lose precious cupcaking time. That's why we rely on store-bought cake mix for our projects. We doctor the mix with buttermilk for flavor and add an egg to improve the structure. In addition to the perfect cake mix recipe, we have given you nine variations, adding extra ingredients to the different mixes. Feel free to use your favorite mixes, but avoid lighter ones like angel food or chiffon cake because they sink. If you have a favorite "scratch" recipe, go ahead and use it. To save time, we often make our cupcakes the day before, wrap them in plastic, and decorate them the next day. They stay nice and moist in the plastic wrap overnight.

We use store-bought frosting right out of the can for most projects. Store-bought frosting tints well, creating strong, vibrant colors, and it is the only frosting we trust for melting and dipping. But not all store-bought frostings are created equal. Make sure you avoid ones that are whipped, low-fat, or low-sugar; they don't hold up.

When we have more time or just want to be able to say, "It's homemade," we turn to our own Almost-Homemade Buttercream, the base from which all our other flavors are built. We've given you eight flavors, all of them delicious, plus an almost-instant ganache for creating rich, shiny surfaces.

We have also included two recipes for working with store-bought refrigerated cookie dough. The simple addition of some flour or cocoa powder creates a dough that is easy to work with and bakes into nice firm cookies.

Cupcakes

Perfect Cake Mix Cupcakes   220

Chocolate Chunk Surprise   221

Chocolate-Mint   221

Banana-Chocolate   221

Spice-Rum   221

Double-Top Banana   222

Pumpkin-Spice   222

Strawberry Supreme   222

Orange-Spice   222

Gingerbread   222

Frostings

Almost-Homemade Vanilla Buttercream   223

Orange Buttercream   224

Ginger-Spice Buttercream   224

Espresso Buttercream   224

Raspberry Buttercream   224

Nutella Buttercream   224

Peanut Butter Buttercream   224

Honey Buttercream   224

Next-to-Instant Ganache   224

Cookies

Quick Sugar Cookies   225

Chocolate Sugar Cookies   225

PERFECT CAKE MIX CUPCAKES

Avoid cake mixes with pudding in the mix and lighter kinds such as angel food, since cupcaking requires firm cake. If you don't have buttermilk on hand, you can make a fair substitution by adding 1 tablespoon lemon juice to 1 cup whole milk. Let stand for 10 minutes to sour (real buttermilk is better).

1 box (18.25 ounces) cake mix (such as classic vanilla or devil's food)

1 cup buttermilk (in place of the water called for on the box)

Vegetable oil (the amount on the box)

4 large eggs (in place of the number called for on the box)

1. Preheat the oven to 350°F. Line muffin cups with paper liners.

2. Following the box's instructions, combine all the ingredients in a large bowl, using the buttermilk in place of the water specified (the box will call for more water than the buttermilk here), using the amount of vegetable oil that is called for (typically, white or yellow cake calls for $\frac{1}{3}$ cup; chocolate cakes usually call for $\frac{1}{2}$ cup), and adding the 4 eggs. Beat with an electric mixer until moistened, about 30 seconds. Increase the speed to high and beat until thick, 2 minutes longer.

3. Spoon half of the batter into a large ziplock bag, press out the excess air, and seal. Snip a $\frac{1}{4}$-inch corner from the bag and fill the paper liners two-thirds full (see page 10). Repeat with the remaining batter. Bake until golden (if using a light-colored cake mix) and a toothpick inserted in the center comes out clean, 20 to 25 minutes for jumbo, 15 to 20 minutes for standard, and 8 to 10 minutes for mini cupcakes. Remove the cupcakes from the baking pans, place on a wire rack, and allow to cool completely.

CHOCOLATE CHUNK SURPRISE

- 1 box (18.25 ounces) devil's food cake mix
- 1 cup buttermilk
- $1/2$ cup vegetable oil
- 4 large eggs
- 12–24 caramel cream–filled chocolates (Milky Way Minis; halve if making mini cupcakes)

Make as directed on page 220, submerging a caramel cream–filled chocolate into each muffin cup filled with batter.

CHOCOLATE-MINT

- 1 box (18.25 ounces) devil's food cake mix
- 1 cup buttermilk
- $1/2$ cup vegetable oil
- 4 large eggs
- $3/4$ cup chopped mint chocolates (Andes Crème de Menthe Thins)

Make as directed on page 220, folding the chopped mint chocolates into the batter.

BANANA-CHOCOLATE

- 1 box (18.25 ounces) devil's food cake mix
- 1 cup mashed bananas (about 3 medium)
- $3/4$ cup buttermilk
- $1/2$ cup vegetable oil
- 4 large eggs

Make as directed on page 220, adding the mashed bananas with the buttermilk and oil.

SPICE-RUM

- 1 box (18.25 ounces) spice cake mix
- 2 tablespoons minced crystallized ginger
- 1 teaspoon ground ginger
- $1/2$ teaspoon ground cinnamon
- $1/4$ teaspoon ground nutmeg
  Pinch ground cloves
- 1 teaspoon rum extract
- 1 cup buttermilk
- $1/3$ cup vegetable oil
- 4 large eggs

Make as directed on page 220, adding the minced ginger and spices to the cake mix and adding the rum extract with the buttermilk and oil.

DOUBLE-TOP BANANA

- 1 box (18.25 ounces) banana supreme cake mix
- 1 cup mashed bananas (about 3 medium)
- 2/3 cup buttermilk
- 1/3 cup vegetable oil
- 4 large eggs

Make as directed on page 220, adding the mashed bananas with the buttermilk and oil.

PUMPKIN-SPICE

- 1 box (18.25 ounces) classic vanilla cake mix
- 1 cup canned pumpkin (not pumpkin pie filling)
- 1 teaspoon pumpkin pie spice
- 3/4 cup buttermilk
- 1/3 cup vegetable oil
- 4 large eggs

Make as directed on page 220, adding the canned pumpkin and pumpkin pie spice with the buttermilk and oil.

STRAWBERRY SUPREME

- 1 box (18.25 ounces) strawberry supreme cake mix
- 1 cup buttermilk
- 1/3 cup vegetable oil
- 4 large eggs

Make as directed on page 220.

ORANGE-SPICE

- 1 box (18.25 ounces) classic vanilla cake mix
- 1 cup buttermilk
- 1/3 cup vegetable oil
- 4 large eggs
- 2 teaspoons pumpkin pie spice
- 1/2 teaspoon grated orange peel

Make as directed on page 220, stirring the pumpkin pie spice and orange peel into the batter.

GINGERBREAD

- 1 box (18.25 ounces) classic vanilla cake mix
- 1/2 cup buttermilk
- 1/2 cup molasses
- 1/3 cup vegetable oil
- 4 large eggs
- 1 1/2 teaspoons ground ginger
- 1/2 teaspoon ground cinnamon
- 1/4 teaspoon ground nutmeg

Make as directed on page 220, adding the molasses and spices with the buttermilk and oil.

FROSTINGS

ALMOST-HOMEMADE VANILLA BUTTERCREAM

3 sticks (³/₄ pound) unsalted butter, cut into 1-inch pieces and softened

1 container (16 ounces) Marshmallow Fluff

¹/₂ cup confectioners' sugar, plus more if desired

1 teaspoon vanilla extract

1. Beat the butter in a large mixing bowl with an electric mixer on medium speed until light and fluffy. Add the Marshmallow Fluff and beat until smooth, scraping down the sides of the bowl. Add the confectioners' sugar and vanilla extract and beat until light and fluffy. If the mixture seems too stiff, soften in the microwave for no more than 10 seconds and beat well again until smooth.

2. Add up to 1 cup more confectioners' sugar to taste, if desired.

ORANGE BUTTERCREAM

1 teaspoon grated orange peel

Make as directed, beating in the orange peel until well blended.

GINGER-SPICE BUTTERCREAM

1 tablespoon finely minced crystallized ginger

1/2 teaspoon pumpkin pie spice

1/4 teaspoon ground ginger

Make as directed, beating in the crystallized ginger, pumpkin pie spice, and ground ginger until well blended.

ESPRESSO BUTTERCREAM

4 teaspoons instant espresso powder

1 tablespoon warm water

Make as directed, dissolving the espresso powder in the warm water and beating in until well blended.

RASPBERRY BUTTERCREAM

1/2 cup seedless raspberry jam

Make as directed, beating in the raspberry jam until well blended.

NUTELLA BUTTERCREAM

1/2 cup Nutella

Make as directed, beating in the Nutella until well blended.

PEANUT BUTTER BUTTERCREAM

1/2 cup creamy peanut butter

Make as directed, beating in the peanut butter until well blended.

HONEY BUTTERCREAM

1/4 cup honey

Make as directed, beating in the honey until well blended.

NEXT-TO-INSTANT GANACHE
Makes about 1 1/2 cups

1 can (16 ounces) chocolate or dark chocolate frosting

Spoon the frosting into a micro-wavable 2-cup measuring cup. Microwave on high, stopping to stir frequently, until the frosting has the texture of lightly whipped cream, 30 to 60 seconds.

QUICK SUGAR COOKIES

³/₄ cup all-purpose flour

1 tube (16.5 ounces) refrigerated sugar cookie dough

1. Preheat the oven to 350°F. Line two cookie sheets with parchment paper.

2. Knead the flour into the dough on a clean work surface until smooth. Divide the dough in half. Roll out each piece on a lightly floured surface to a ¹/₄-inch thickness. Cut out the desired shapes according to the recipe, cutting as close together as possible, using templates or a homemade cookie cutter. Transfer the shapes to the prepared pans, spacing about 1 inch apart. Remove the center areas of the cookies if directed in the recipe.

3. Bake until golden and firm to the touch, 7 to 12 minutes depending on the size and shape of the cookies. Transfer to a wire rack and cool completely.

CHOCOLATE SUGAR COOKIES

¹/₃ cup all-purpose flour

¹/₄ cup unsweetened cocoa powder

1 tube (16.5 ounces) refrigerated sugar cookie dough

1. Preheat the oven to 350°F. Line two cookie sheets with parchment paper.

2. Knead the flour and cocoa powder into the dough on a clean work surface until smooth. Divide the dough in half. Roll out each piece on a lightly floured surface to a ¹/₄-inch thickness. Cut out the desired shapes according to the recipe, cutting as close together as possible, using templates or a homemade cookie cutter. Transfer the shapes to the prepared pans, spacing about 1 inch apart. Remove the center areas of the cookies if directed in the recipe.

3. Bake until golden and firm to the touch, 7 to 12 minutes depending on the size and shape of the cookies. Transfer to a wire rack and cool completely.

SOURCES

BAKING SUPPLIES

Ateco
(800) 645-7170
www.atecousa.net
Offset spatulas. *A good source for cake decorating tools.*

Beryl's
P.O. Box 1584
North Springfield, VA 22151
(703) 256-6951
(800) 488-2749
www.beryls.com
A wide variety of cupcake paper liners, as well as many other cupcake decorating supplies.

Cake Mate
www.cakemate.com
A complete list of sugar and sprinkles available at your local grocery store, as well as creative cupcake ideas.

Confectionery House
(518) 279-4250
(518) 279-3179
www.confectioneryhouse.com
Solid-color cupcake paper liners. *A wide variety of melting chocolate wafers, sprinkles, food coloring, and luster dust.*

Country Kitchen SweetArt
4621 Speedway Drive
Fort Wayne, IN 46825
(260) 482-4835
(800) 497-3927
www.countrykitchensa.com
Sanding and coarse sugars. *A wide variety of candy decors, sprinkles, luster dust, chocolate melting wafers, food coloring, and paper liners.*

Duncan Hines
www.duncanhines.com
A complete list of cake mixes and frostings available at your local grocery store, as well as creative cupcake ideas and tips and ideas for baking.

Fancy Flours
www.fancyflours.com
Beautiful and elegant cupcake supplies, from paper liners to specialty sugars, sprinkles, and decorations.

India Tree Gourmet Spices & Specialties
1421 Elliott Avenue West
Seattle, WA 98119
(206) 270-0293
(800) 369-4848
www.indiatree.com
Beautiful coarse and decorating sugars. India Tree products are also available in some grocery stores.

Kitchen Krafts
P.O. Box 442
Waukon, IA 52172
(563) 535-8000
(800) 298-5389
www.kitchenkrafts.com
A wide variety of decorating supplies.

McCormick
www.mccormick.com
A great source for large-size food coloring and hard-to-find colors like neon and black and a strong selection of seasonal cupcake ideas. The color wheel on the food-color section of the website makes it easy to create custom colors.

New York Cake & Baking Supplies
56 West 22nd Street
New York, NY 10010
(212) 675-2253
N.Y. Cake West
10665 W. Pico Blvd.
Los Angeles, CA 90064
(310) 481-0875
(877) NY-CAKE-8
www.nycake.com
Food coloring, chocolate melting wafers, luster dust, dragées, sugars, sprinkles, and some paper liners.

Sugarcraft
2715 Dixie Highway
Hamilton, OH 45015
(513) 896-7089
www.sugarcraft.com
A wide variety of baking and decorating supplies.

Sur La Table
(800) 243-0852
www.surlatable.com
Crinkle cutters. *Bakeware, tiered cake stands, and schedules of decorating classes at stores.*

Wilton Industries
2240 West 75th Street
Woodbridge, IL 60517
(630) 963-1818
(800) 794-5866
www.wilton.com
A wide variety of baking supplies, including chocolate melting wafers, food coloring, paper liners, assorted sprinkles and sugars, and much more. Wilton products are also available in many craft and party stores and some grocery stores.

PARTY AND CRAFT SUPPLIES

A.C. Moore
www.acmoore.com
Marvy paper punch, plastic eggs. *Cake-decorating supplies and crafts, as well as books. Store locations are listed online.*

Beadalon
www.beadalon.com
Offset tweezers. *A great source for sorting trays and crafting mats.*

Fiskars
www.fiskars.com
Craft scissors. *Creative craft ideas, seminars, and products.*

Fred & Friends
www.worldwidefred.com
Finger Food plates. Also other novelty items. Store locations are listed online.

Michael's Craft Stores
(800) 642-4235
www.michaels.com
Marvy paper punch, plastic eggs. *A wide variety of craft supplies and cake-decorating supplies, including Wilton products.*

Paper Source
www.paper-source.com
Beautiful papers and crafting supplies, packing material, and boxes for cupcake gifts.

Reynolds
www.reynoldskitchens.com
The latest seasonal paper and foil liner selections, as well as a selection of creative cupcake ideas.

Tower Hobbies, K&S Brass Supplies
(217) 398-3636
(800) 637-6050
www.towerhobbies.com
Thin brass strips for making cookie cutters. *Other craft supplies.*

Ziploc
www.ziploc.com
Product information, as well as coupons for Ziploc products.

GOURMET CANDY SUPPLIES

Balboa Candy
301-A Marine Avenue
Balboa Island, CA 92662
(949) 723-6099
www.balboacandy.com
A great candy selection, specializing in retro candies and taffy.

Bulk Candy Store
(877) 392-2639
www.bulkcandystore.com
White and pastel colored circus peanuts. *Candies of all kinds, available in bulk size as well as smaller bags.*

Dylan's Candy Bar
1011 Third Avenue
New York, NY 10021
(866) 9-DYLANS
www.dylanscandybar.com
A wide variety of candies, including seasonal offerings.

Economy Candy
108 Rivington Street
New York, NY 10002
(800) 352-4544
www.economycandy.com
A good source for old-fashioned and bulk candies.

Jelly Belly Candy Company
One Jelly Belly Lane
Fairfield, CA 94533
(800) JB-BEANS
www.jellybelly.com
The largest selection available of gourmet jelly beans, including bulk sizes of individual flavors. The website includes a selection of creative cupcake ideas.

Old Time Candy Company
(866) WAX-LIPS
www.oldtimecandy.com
An interesting selection of nostalgic and novelty candies; large or small quantities can be purchased.

Sunflower Food & Spice Company
13318 West 99th Street
Lenexa, KS 66215
(913) 599-6448
(800) 377-4693
www.sunflowerfood
company.com
Sunny Seed Drops. *A wide variety of colors of candy-coated chocolate-covered sunflower seeds.*

Sweet Factory
2000 East Winston Road
Anaheim, CA 92806
(877) 817-9338
www.sweetfactory.com
A great selection of hard-to-find candies. Online and retail locations nationwide.

CUPCAKE INDEX

Faux Food (April Fool's) Cupcakes
Side of Fries (EZ), 23–25
Bagels and Lox (EZ), 26–27
Hold the Anchovies, 28–30
Faux Foot-Long, 31–34
All Cracked Up, 35–37
Corn on the Cob (EZ), 38–39
Spaghetti and Meatballs (EZ),
 40–41
Bake-Sale Pies, 42–43
Chinese Takeout, 44–48
Banana Split, 49–51

Birthday Cupcakes
Ring Bling, 53–56
Fur Balls and String Monsters (EZ),
 57–59
Formula One Cupcakes, 60–64
Flower Power, 65–67
Karaoke Cupcakes (EZ), 68–69
Slumber Party, 70–73
Artist's Palette (EZ), 74–75
Robocup, 76–78
Jungle Fever, 79–83

Animal Cupcakes
Chocolate Moose, 85–88
Hound Dogs, 89–91
March of the Penguins, 92–95
Westies, 96–98
Koi Pond (EZ), 99–101
Ants on a Picnic (EZ), 102–3
Busy Bees, 104–7
Shark Attack!, 108–12
Crazy Horses, 113–15

Party Cupcakes
I'm Seeing a Pattern, 117–19
An Apple a Day, 120–22
Sunflowers (EZ), 123–25
Sweet Talk, 126–28
Rubber Ducky, 129–31
Baby Shower, 132–35
Easter Eggs, 136–38
Garden Party, 139–43
Mum's the Word (EZ), 144–45
Head of the Class, 146–48
Nineteenth Hole (EZ), 149–51

**Halloween and Thanksgiving
Cupcakes**
The Haunted House, 153–56
Chilly Ghosts (EZ), 157–59
Alien Invasion, 160–62
Creepy Crawlers, 163–65
What a Hoot! (EZ), 167–69
Jack-O'-Lanterns (EZ), 170–73
Mr. Bones Jangle, 174–76
Howling Werewolves, 177–79
Black Cats, 180–82
Larry the Turkey, 183–85

**Christmas and
Hanukkah Cupcakes**
Eye-Candy Ornaments,
 187–89
Edible Ornaments, 190–92
Gingerbread Boys (EZ), 193–95
Punch-Drunk Elves, 196–99
Blue Poinsettias (EZ), 200–1
Frosty Mugs (EZ), 202–3
Oh Tannenbaum, 204–7
Polar Bears, 208–10
White Wreath, 211–13
Gingerbread Village, 214–17

After a While, Crocodile!

Karen Tack is the coauthor of the *New York Times* best-selling books *Hello, Cupcake!* and *What's New, Cupcake?* She is a cooking teacher and a food stylist and has created cupcakes and other desserts for the covers of many of America's top magazines, including *Bon Appétit, Gourmet, Cook's Illustrated, Good Housekeeping, Family Circle, Every Day with Rachael Ray, Woman's Day, Martha Stewart Living, Parents, Real Simple, FamilyFun,* and *All You.*

Alan Richardson is the coauthor of the *New York Times* best-selling books *Hello, Cupcake!* and *What's New, Cupcake?* He is also the coauthor of *The Breath of a Wok,* which won two prestigious awards from the International Association of Culinary Professionals (IACP). His photographs appear in dozens of best-selling cookbooks and leading food magazines.

OUR WEBSITE

www.hellocupcakebook.com
www.whatsnewcupcake.com

Visit our website to see our latest cupcake designs, to get information on the newest candies, as well as updates on demonstrations, events, and book signings, and to fill us in on your own cupcaking adventures.

Follow us on Twitter (@whatsnewcupcake) to hear what we are saying about cupcakes right now.